Ovid's Erotic Poems

Ovid's Erotic Poems

Amores
AND
Ars Amatoria

TRANSLATED BY
Len Krisak

INTRODUCTION BY
Sarah Ruden

PENN

University of Pennsylvania Press

Philadelphia

Published by
University of Pennsylvania Press
Philadelphia, Pennsylvania 19104-4112

Printed in the United States of America on acid-free paper
1 3 5 7 9 10 8 6 4 2

Library of Congress Cataloging-in-Publication Data

Ovid, 43 B.C.–17 A.D. or 18 A.D.
[Amores. English]
Ovid's erotic poems : "Amores" and "Ars amatoria" / translated by Len Krisak ;
introduction by Sarah Ruden. — 1st ed.
       p.   cm.
ISBN 978-0-8122-4625-4 (hardcover : alk. paper)
1. Love poetry, Latin—Translations into English. 2. Erotic poetry, Latin—
Translations into English. I. Krisak, Len, 1948– II. Ovid, 43 B.C.–17 A.D.
or 18 A.D. Ars amatoria. English. III. Title: Ars amatoria.
                PA6522.A3   2014b
        871'.01—dc23
                            2014012364

CONTENTS

INTRODUCTION

I T IS A STRANGE THOUGH CRITICAL IRONY THAT OVID (43 B.C.E.–17 C.E.), the ancient world's greatest love poet, has a reputation for outstanding frivolity, particularly in his fundamental erotic works, the *Amores* (Loves) and *Ars Amatoria* (The Art of Love). Frivolity and romantic love don't match up very well in our minds.

But from one angle that characterization makes sense. Ovid is one of our richest sources on *otium*, literally "leisure," and in Rome the word was particularly suggestive of things that are extra, ephemeral, disposable—such as the love affairs a young man might indulge in as long as they did not involve serious infatuation that might distract him from duties and prescribed ambitions. Every relationship Ovid depicts comes under the heading of dalliance: any assertion of real, lasting emotional involvement is canceled out by the poet's satirical wit.

His persona's involvement with a woman whom he calls Corinna in the *Amores* amounts to little but a series of clichés brilliantly undercut: the lover constantly protests his helplessness, for example, but his superb rhetorical control in itself makes that protest ridiculous. He is far more interested in declaiming on stock themes such as the wickedness of sailing, and in creating dramatizations in which Corinna—or another woman, or more than one—is a mere prop. In Book II, Poem

II of the *Amores*, Corinna is about to go to sea, and he protests her decision and prays for her safety in fifty-six allusive lines that would be absurdly pretentious if he meant a word of them.

Ars Amatoria, for its part, is a parody in its very form, that of didactic verse. Two long, discursive books instruct men on the science of selecting a woman, flirting with her, handling her—then, briefly, how to please her in bed. A third book tells women how to handle their side of the romantic confidence game. Again, spicing up what by this time had become the pabulum of literary eroticism is Ovid's prevailing technique.

Ovid's love poetry is therefore the antithesis of *negotium* and its literature. *Negotium* was almost the defining condition for respectable men of the citizen class. I prefer to translate the word according to its etymology, as "non-leisure" rather than "business," because it covers everything someone would do to advance his interests in the public sphere. First, there were private commercial dealings, politics, and public administration, often jumbled together—all three were based on rhetoric, or the science of speaking and writing. Witness the orator Cicero's mammoth yet exquisitely crafted personal correspondence that complements his published speeches and treatises. But *negotium* included even literary avocations such as writing history or poetry, a rather shocking example of which was Cicero's (now mercifully lost) epic poem *De consulatu suo* (On His [Own] Consulship), celebrating his alleged heroism in Rome's highest public office. The literature of *negotium* purported to show a man at his real, solid best.

The literature of *otium* seems to have emerged only a generation or two before Ovid and is first extant in the work of the poet Catullus (who died, young, in the mid-fifties B.C.E.). Ovid's erotic poetry represents—to my mind, anyway—the ancient world's tightest combination of delight in the world with delight in writing. He is by far the keenest observer of early Imperial Rome's details, and the wittiest confabulator to use this material, from the look and sound of public entertainments to the mechanics of recreational sex, and from the distant spectacles of large historical events to the moods in an apartment where a courtesan tries a new hairstyle to better suit the shape of her face or fights for her life after an abortion.

But even though some of the topics are still customarily called "light," the term "frivolous" is unfair: at this stage of his career (as opposed to his time of exile after 8 c.e., when loneliness, humiliation, and a campaign to be recalled produced what can look like real personal writing), Ovid is not concerned with anything so trivial as his own physical desires or emotional attachments, or even his own wider circumstances or experiences. Even his career as a roué may have been fictional or brief, given what he writes in exile in the collections entitled *Tristia* (Sad Things) and *Letters from Pontus* (the Black Sea, beside which he made his involuntary new home) about his loving, loyal, desperately missed third wife, whom he probably married around the age of thirty, when many Roman men contracted their *first* legal unions).

But in the texts of the *Amores* and *Ars Amatoria* themselves lies the main evidence that Ovid's love poetry was about itself, so that his freedom and achievement there went far beyond the necessary narrow limits of self-depiction or self-expression: it was creation in a broader sense that concerned him, creation feeding on the infinity of literary possibilities rather than the decidedly finite store of individual human experience. The writing luxuriates in rhetorical convolutions and send-ups of the love elegy genre that it technically inhabits, and is obviously determined to use all its contents as mere combustible material for verbal and dramatic fireworks.

But in a stunt such as this, the indispensable thing, the thing that prevents the composition from being a mere pile of dry tiresomeness that over time will grow soggy and rot, is the spark of genius. If genius is above all the ability to create a new world, then Ovid is one of literature's great geniuses; and if the genius of modernity is above all independent, individual creation, then Ovid is the foundational modern mind. Authors of all kinds had come before him, but in my opinion he was the first writer, and the erotic poetry seems a fitting prelude to the first writerly masterpiece, his epic *Metamorphoses*, in which the whole range of Greek and Roman mythology is a mere playground for his narrative skill.

Ovid's Life

This poet's biography, plausibly presented in one of his exile poems, looks at the beginning a good deal like that of a typical Roman author of the Republican Era, which ended when Ovid was still a child. His family belonged to the wealthy, land-owning Italian aristocracy and sent him to Rome to distinguish himself first as a student of famous rhetoricians and then as an advocate in the law courts and as a politician. Much later in life, he asserted that his undeniable natural impulse was toward poetry, and that this was the reason he shunned a political career, but he very likely perceived early on that politics was no longer the best choice for a really ambitious man.

Though the senate, the popular assembly, and the law courts met as usual, important policy in these new Imperial times was decided within the emperor's household, leaving orators in the public sphere to speak only on cue and to excite no one. No wonder Ovid evinced a stubborn interest in another branch of literature than political or forensic rhetoric. And given the opportunities a previous generation of poets had found to be celebrated in their own right (though their voices were hardly autonomous), no wonder this branch was poetry.

This was because of the patronage of a remarkable man. Caesar Octavian, ruling under the title Augustus (roughly, "the Man Who

Is the Source of Growth," with sacral overtones), had ended a hundred years of on-and-off civil wars. After his decisive victory in the Battle of Actium (31 B.C.E.) allowed him to take control of Rome's political system as the first of the Roman emperors, he propagandized—partly though poets—that under Roman governance the world was now beginning a golden age of peace and prosperity. This news, of course, would have made little impression had he not been a supremely able administrator.

The most solid and lasting evidence of Augustus's skill and judgment survives from his literary program. Employing his highly cultured friends Maecenas and Messalla as talent scouts, he fostered several geniuses, apparently never snubbing obscure origins or an uncongenial political past. Horace (65–8 B.C.E.) was actually the son of a freed slave and had fought in the losing Republic army against the forces of Julius Caesar, the new emperor's adoptive father and quasi-predecessor. Nonetheless, under Augustus's auspices and Maecenas's management Horace was funded, defended, and not overtaxed with demands for court poetry. Another poet was Virgil, and it is arguable that his career could not even have started without the emperor's help.

Perhaps in part because Augustus was firmly settled in power and less in need of kudos by the time of Ovid's early maturity, or perhaps because Ovid's inherited status was higher, or perhaps simply because of his innate independence of mind, the poet's erotic verses have a very different tone from that of anything by his older colleagues. Though Ovid was ostensibly pro-Augustan, his support was expressed in such flip connections that he must not have felt any great pressure to propagandize, or even to avoid constant irony about the very existence of the public sphere, which he depicts mainly as a stage for flirtation. An anticipated Triumph (a grandiose parade celebrating a major military victory) by a young relative and protégé of Augustus, reports Ovid in

Book I of the *Ars Amatoria*, will be an ideal occasion for picking up a girl; a man on the make can plant himself next to one and identify each part of the pageant representing conquered places, peoples, and leaders:

> Tell her everything, and not just if you're bid;
> If you don't know, respond as if you did.   (I.221–222)

The content and tone of the erotic poetry is one basis for debate about the most intriguing juncture in Ovid's life. In 8 c.e. he found Augustus to be something other than a benevolent dictator and patron of the arts. There is no way to know the precise nature of the poet's indiscretions—as tantalizingly cited by himself in *Tristia* 2.207 as *carmen et error*, "a poem and a mistake"—that brought this change about (though Augustus's daughter Julia, notoriously promiscuous, is a good candidate for involvement, and a conspiracy within the imperial household was harshly repressed around the time Ovid was banished), but whatever happened was so enraging to the emperor that it saw the poet exiled to the hardscrabble outpost of Tomis (modern Constanta, in Romania), toward the far end of the Black Sea. Ovid pleaded in hundreds of lines of exile poetry to be allowed to return, but Augustus's anger was implacable—or more than implacable, as it survived his death, to keep Ovid at his immense distance from the Roman metropolis until the poet's own death three years later.

How could the emperor resist such appeals? Ovid's poetic reports swell with images of the wild, barren, freezing country he has landed in and the dangers to the fortified outpost from attacking barbarians, whose poisoned arrows land in the street and stick in the roofs. But making the best of it, he learns (or so he claims) the local language well enough to compose a poem about the apotheosis of Augustus (imperial propaganda ascribed to him divine ancestry and a heavenly destiny); the locals, hearing a recitation, are sure (according to Ovid) that this will win a summons home. Interestingly, grave as the offense must have been to have brought a punishment this harsh and inescapable, the scandal never broke—into the historical record, that is. Perhaps the permanent exile of a popular, well-connected poet served mainly as a warning and helped keep the facts hushed up.

In any case, Ovid's several mentions of his erotic poetry as forming part of Augustus's motivation are probably little more than an attempt to throw readers off the trail. If Augustus did object to the admittedly irreverent poems, then why hadn't he done anything when they were published in at least one version each—we're not certain at what point that was, but at least six years earlier than the blow-up immediately before the exile? Why had it not been sufficient for Ovid to have carefully dismissed married women, in words reminiscent of religious prohibition, from among his pupils at the beginning of *Ars Amatoria* (I.31–43)? This would seem to correct poems in the earlier work, the *Amores* (such as the entire Poem I.4), that could be deemed disrespectful to Augustus's morals legislation. These laws were aimed in part at adulterous wives and their corruptors—but not at men roving at large, nor at sex professionals, and the two categories seem to comprise the usual actors in Ovid's scenarios. Not only sporting eroticism but also literary eroticism were sanctioned diversions for men. A statesman as proper as Cicero leaves us an example of the latter, cited with amused indulgence by another statesman, Pliny the Younger, more than a century later. At worst, Ovid's taste for publicity was problematic, as the normal forum for "trifles" and "jokes" concerning sex was the private dinner party.

Moreover, though Ovid may have been best known for his love poetry, his output as a whole speaks of a learned eclecticism that should have done the regime proud. His first extant book (the *Heroides*) comprised love letters of mythological characters, and, besides assorted minor works, he also produced a tragedy (*Medea*, now lost), an unfinished collection of Roman lore (the *Fasti*) based on the calendar, and of course the *Metamorphoses*. If Augustus did suddenly turn censor, it was in the spirit of "You're no good! I should have known it back when you did X, but I'm certain of it now that you've done Y." Without Y, there would never have been an outburst about anything.

Erotic Poetry and Elegy in Greece and Rome

Love poetry was quite a late development in the ancient world. At least in oral form, epic poetry dates back for millennia, and of course it contains erotic elements. For example, the *Odyssey* (VIII.266ff.) features the tale of the adulterous lovers Aphrodite and Ares caught naked in an invisible net rigged over the goddess's bed. But it was not until the late seventh century B.C.E. on the island of Lesbos that someone emerged as a love poet. This was of course Sappho with her lyrical outpourings.

The circumstances of her writing remain disputed, but the surviving fragments give the same impression to us as the complete poems did to the ancients: the poet is frankly helpless against her passions, which can be like a form of madness. Roughly five hundred years later, the Roman poet Catullus (Poem 51) imitated her most famous poem, about a seizure brought on watching a man and a woman—who is addressed in the first person—as the woman talks and laughs with him. (We also have the original Greek version quoted in the treatise *On the Sublime*, attributed to a critic called Longinus.) Folklore had long held that Sappho died by hurling herself into the sea, because of unrequited love for a young man.

Catullus's special homage—apparently the only poem of his that is close to a word-for-word translation of a predecessor—is apt. He is the first Roman we could call a love poet in the mode of Sappho, and we have plausible historical accounts of his unhappy love affair, including a name: it was Clodia, the wife of the consul (one of two Roman yearly heads of state) Metellus, to whom he gives the pseudonym Lesbia (*not* meaning "lesbian," which was not at the time the emphasis in Sappho's reputation: though she reports emotional involvements with women, her memory merely evoked the transports of love—and the delights of literature).

But a word of caution is in order for those who might think that Greek and Roman erotic poets were similar to troubadours, modern love poets, or pop balladeers. Even for Sappho and Catullus, the erotic poets most likely to have spoken sincerely and personally, the work shows literary functions far removed from simple self-expression, one-to-one communication, or even the publicizing of either of these. For example, in asserting the power of love, Sappho uses an *exemplum*, or invocation of authority from the literary tradition, and here at least this is the lofty, almost abstract tradition of epic. She picks out one character from the *Iliad*, Helen, and describes the Trojan War's precipitating crisis from her point of view: Helen left her royal husband and her young child behind to follow her lover Paris to Troy (Fragment 16).

The common modern critical explanation is that Sappho re-forms mythology to testify to a woman's special interests, as a sort of protest, but this makes little sense. For one thing, though some minds (like Ovid's, certainly) could be more independent than others, there tended to be no clean delineation between an individual's inner sense of self and a sense of the self's outward endowments obtained from education, clan, religion, culture, and nationality, and traditional stories inhered in all of these. Even the poets we might call not erotic but pornographic had no actual ability to set themselves apart from society and claim, "That's society over there; here I am in defiance of it." The one exception is Archilochus (early seventh century B.C.E.); perhaps because as an illegitimate son, a mercenary, and a colonist at a time when Greece was emerging from its dark ages, he was that almost unknown phenomenon in the ancient world: an outsider with a standard education.

In contrast, though Catullus howls about his girlfriend's betrayals—and a speech extant from the murder trial of one of her lovers provides some evidence that he had plenty to howl about—he does it in strict, rarified meter inherited from the great lyric poets of Greece, and his emotion is no less raw when displaced into a female mythological heroine, Ariadne standing in disarray on a lonely sea shore and lamenting her abandonment by Theseus (Poem 64).

Interestingly, this poem is not a lyric but a "little epic," in dactylic hexameters. Erotic subject matter in epic both relatively short and of the full traditional length had been favored among the learned Alexandrian poets in Egypt and its surrounds, between the Greek Classical period and the Roman literary ascendancy. This phenomenon crystallizes some important differences between ancient erotic poetry and our own, differences I have already stressed: ancient erotic poetry had profound debts to learned tradition, and this kept it relatively impersonal—more in the character of artifact than of documentation. Beyond that, it was hardly ever a practical tool such as a message or a gift to a real beloved. Shakespeare's sonnets or Elizabeth Barrett Browning's *Sonnets from the Portuguese* are nothing like what the ancient erotic poets were up to. In their environment, it was easier than it would have been elsewhere for Ovid to transcend toward pure language and pure imagination.

At any rate, in erotic poetry's evolution, elegiac couplets must have been an apt mediating form where the tension between the personal and public needed balancing over long works—that is, when erotic poetry had developed to the point where long, almost novelistic works became possible. This began in Greece around 400 B.C.E. with the poet and dramatist Antimachus, whose lost poem *Lyde* made literary myths the vehicle for a lament over a beloved's death. The genre flowered in Rome under Augustus, when three writers were known mainly or exclusively as love elegists: Gallus (very little of whose work is extant), Propertius, and Tibullus.

Propertius begins his collection with the line "Cynthia was the first to capture poor me with her [sweet little] eyes," and proceeds to narrate the ups and downs (mostly downs) of the love affair; Tibullus features two girlfriends, Delia and Nemesis. The poems, like Ovid's *Amores*, are dozens of lines long, and like them constitute vignettes or episodes; together, they are a sort of story, but without the linear narrative drive of a novel. There are various stock scenes and situations: a blissful, too-short night together; clandestine correspondence; the threat of a rival; the lover is locked outside the beloved's house at night; he renounces a military career to serve in love's army; the girl's shallow or outright mercenary character or influences send him into despair; and so on. Some of these tropes go back at least to Greek Old Comedy and are rife in the early Roman theater of Plautus and Terence. The lover's speeches on familiar topics, including Beauty Unadorned, Old-Time Piety, and Virtuous Poverty, link the genre to the philosophical schools and the practice of declamation, or display rhetoric.

A special feature of love elegy was the concentration on a single woman and the evolution of her relationship with the narrator. As with Catullus's Lesbia playing with a pet bird and then mourning its death (Poems 2 and 3), we get a sense of a living personality, and the poet's infatuation is credible. Cynthia and Delia, it might be said, are *more* convincing than if we saw them only through a man's lovesick mind. They don't retreat quickly and irrevocably from idealization into the obscurity of resentment and estrangement; they come and go, and their moods and circumstances change realistically. They don't disappear when their admirer isn't there but have independent occupations such as religious observances and visits among women friends, and they display their own learning and tastes. Here, where the female protagonists are probably for the most part fictional, their roles cohere and convince. In Augustan Rome, with its army of courtesans who were both consumers and consumed, cultured and part of *the* culture in the first really well-established imperial society, a form of literature became popular that still rings true.

Elegiac meter is an excellent vehicle for this achievement. The meter consists of an indefinite series of couplets, the first line of each being the same as an epic hexameter, or six-foot unit. The basic schema of the hexameter is the following, with one long (—) and two short syllables (∪∪) making up each foot but the last:

$$—\cup\cup \mid —\cup\cup \mid —\cup\cup \mid —\cup\cup \mid —\cup\cup \mid — —$$

But most pairs of short syllables can be replaced by a single long one. This is because Latin meter is quantitative, not qualitative, as in English verse. In quantitative meter it takes longer to pronounce some syllables than others, whereas in qualitative meter the rhythm on which the line is built is based on stress, on whether the natural beat in a word falls on a particular syllable or not. The final long syllable of the hexameter can be replaced by a single short one.

It is an organic, flowing meter in Greek and Latin, pausing where the words for a single image or action are likely to pause, and so apt for narrative, as in English, where the often-cited example is Longfellow's "American epic," *Evangeline*:

> This is the forest primeval. The murmuring pines and the hemlocks,
> Bearded with moss, and in garments green, indistinct in the twilight,
> Stand like Druids of eld, with voices sad and prophetic.

But in elegiac couplets the hexameter alternates with a line that has a mandatory, very distinct pause separating the first two-and-one-half feet from the second; these two halves together amount to five feet and give the line its name, "pentameter." This one, with conventional replacement syllables, would be:

$$-\overline{\cup\cup}\mid-\overline{\cup\cup}\mid-\parallel-\overline{\cup\cup}\mid-\cup\cup\mid\overset{\cup}{}$$

The translations in this volume show a rare commitment to reproducing in English the authentic sound of Roman elegiac couplets, and along with it their essential effect, commonly called the "pointed style" of later Roman rhetoric:

> My one-time love, who started up with only me,
>> I see is now Rome's common property.
> Now, stop me, but I'd swear my books produced her fame.
>> And so it is: my Muse spread wide her name.
> I earned this! Why did I proclaim her form and face
>> Until my verse became her marketplace?
>
> *(Amores* III.12.5–10)

As in English heroic couplets, where rhyme packages blank verse into compact but malleable pairs of lines (like Pope's "Know then thyself, presume not God to scan; / The proper study of Mankind is Man"), elegiac verse lends itself to pithiness as well as rhetorical or narrative flow. Typical lyric meters dictate a stanza of a special form, and if the number of stanzas is not limited by the character of the genre (as in a Greek choral ode or a sonnet), the sheer difficulty of a stanza's components is likely to intervene. *Eugene Onegin* aside, it's just about impossible to rattle on and on in sonnets.

But in elegiac couplets, that hybrid form between lyric and epic, you *could* rattle on and on—and at the same time easily draw attention away from the subject matter and to yourself, particularly to your processes of thinking and writing. The pairs of lines, moving forward in measured but unlimited sequence, invite all kinds of play with words and ideas both within and across the pairs. The meter is an ideal form for narrative that comments on itself, like the vignettes in Ovid's *Amores*. It is also good for lively didactic poetry like *Ars Amatoria*. More traditional didactic poems in hexameter date back to Hesiod, mythology and legend and fable being natural concomitants of advice for success in life or in a particular calling, but the didacticism of worldly sophistication needed a framework on which it was easier to hang qualifications, quips, irony, sneers, self-deprecation, and many other kinds of writerly performance.

It was through the elegiac form that Ovid took ancient erotic poetry to its logical conclusion. In our culture, that conclusion would have been of the opposite type, familiar in certain pop phenomena: the flourishes of music and literature have been cut down further and further, from thoughts to emotions to physical sensations and even mere physiological responses: fight, flight, or pursuit. But in Imperial Rome, as a triumph of a poet's pride and will, the personal is pared away more and more severely—under the guise of play—until there is nothing left but his knowledge, skill, and adaptability.

He begins by parodying the investment scene of the great Alexandrian poet Callimachus, who reports that, when as a child he had started to compose epic poetry, Apollo swooped down and forced him to rethink his vocation. Ovid at the start of his poetic career writes one hexameter line of epic—and Cupid steals the final foot of the second line! The poet is annoyed—he doesn't even have a girlfriend. Cupid obligingly shoots him, but doesn't provide an object for his passion. (Corinna, named after a poetaster from Boetia, a Greek land notorious for stupidity, appears only in Poem 3.) Throughout the collection, the lover's stances continue to appear contrarian or trivializing in comparison even to those of his mannered predecessors in love elegy, and he ventures into distinctly unromantic territory in quest of novelty and fun.

Propertius's and Tibullus's beloveds are loveliest when dressed simply and naturally; Ovid writes that he used to rail against Corinna dying her hair, but that's no longer necessary, because one potion caused it all to fall out (I.14). His persona lectures Corinna in lofty philosophical terms as she recovers from a traumatic abortion (II.14). On and on he goes, treating the mere idea of a love affair as a purely intellectual exercise, and lampooning his poetic colleagues who have seemed to take the matter more seriously. Quip by quip, antithesis by mutually annihilating antithesis, he mows his way through sensation, sentiment, and sentimentality, leaving nothing behind but the magic show itself.

Ars Amatoria and its later companion *Remedia Amoris* (*Remedy for Love*, or how to fall *out* of it) take ancient love elegy to the brink of destruction and push it over—and Ovid did kill off the genre by making it impossible for any would-be literary swain to take himself at all seriously. There were in fact no more love poets of any significance, working in any meter, during antiquity, and though the entire Ovidian corpus was exuberantly popular during the Middle Ages, courtly love was built up as a separate edifice on a Christian model: worshipful, self-sacrificing, and tragic.

I think Ovid's final blow to eroticism was his use of the didactic form. Didactic poetry was a lofty undertaking; the greatest Roman example was Lucretius's *On the Nature of the Universe*, a scientific and philosophical account of the world's workings and life's purposes. For didacticism to address love affairs, which for Roman men were supposed to be no more than physical and cultural pleasures, and which for freedwomen were largely a commercial business they understood well enough already, was absurd—and offensive? Not the latter, I think.

Ovid never asserts that he is a serious teacher; as he sets it out, the "successful" sort of "love" is a con game on both sides, which—despite his protests to the contrary—does not even have to be well executed. There is nothing important at stake, and real aptitude would deprive the parties to a love affair—and all the onlookers—of winsome entertainment from the slip-ups he seems to judge inevitable, as they are part of human nature. In one of the funniest passages of ancient literature, *Ars Amatoris* (I.289ff.) illustrates women's innate depravity by showing the mythological queen Pasiphaë, wife of Minos—who in previous accounts was fated through a divine curse to mate with a bull and produce the Minotaur—losing her head for an attractive animal, murderously jealous of her rivals the cows, and scolded by a poet in the voice of an exasperated friend:

> And why a mirror here, where hillside cattle stray?
> > Why rearrange your hair five times a day?
> Believe instead the glass that says you're not a cow.
> > Oh, how you've wished for horns to crown that brow!
> But think of Minos; why begin some mad beguine?
> > At least pick out a *man*; don't be obscene.   (I.305–310)

For Ovid, the ideal of control inhabits another sphere, the sphere of thought and language, and this, in my view, is the chief reason—besides, of course, sheer pleasure—to read him. The *Amores* are, in their essence, a dramatization of undying infatuation with writing, and *The Art of Love* is an instruction book for judging, pursuing, and possessing the art of words.

TRANSLATOR'S PREFACE

INUNDATED BY THE VAST AND CONTRADICTORY LITERATURE on literary translation in general, poetic translation in particular, and the multitudinous seas of theory that swell over these subjects, what is a poor poet to do?

We are told, among various dicta, that to translate at all is to betray or traduce (that tired and by now dreary Italian pun). Or (*pace* Nabokov[1]) we are told that a translation should always be exactly literal, without the slightest deviation from the "true" sense . . . even if the results seem bizarre or off-putting. At the same time, we are also advised that "translationese" (an entity alarmingly like obscenity, in that none of us may be able to define it, but we all certainly know it when we see—that is, hear or read—it) is to be avoided no matter the cost.

By my friends who occasionally succumb to poetic translation (persons who are all highly talented and laureled practitioners of the art of verse), I have been told at various times to do nothing—absolutely nothing—that would harm the English translation as an English poem, no matter what the source language says. But in a sense, isn't what a poem "says" the very heart of the problem in the first place? How can one get over the almost metaphysically difficult hurdle of eliminating all style as a component of both the thought and the total emotional effect of the poem when they are both inextricably bound up in the execution of that style? Isn't the very sound of the words, their physicality and resonance, a nonseparable part of the entire aesthetic experience of verse? Yet certain members of that same fraternity have also advised me that all translation is a waste of time: "Go get Proust and read him in French, and to hell with translations."

I have read, in the thickets of postmodernism, that translation is a poisonous vector of essentialism, an imperialist depredation, a form of colonialist (or postcolonialist?) appropriation, and something to be shunned like Leopold's sins in the Congo.[2] On the other hand, I have also stumbled across the merry thought that maybe none of this matters, so one must write a translation with whatever comes into one's head. After all, the original "authors"—the scare quotes are necessary, I'm afraid—have all been declared dead anyway, and, well, in the case of Ovid, it's pretty clearly true.

In short, the poet faces a welter of contradictory—and therefore unhelpful—advice, ranging from the most academically abstruse to the least theoretical, and a great deal of it fractious.

But *some* decision must at last be made if a poet is to proceed at all, and this seems as good a place as any to lay out an account of my procedure, every step of which bears the inescapable marks of some form of belief about the nature of poetic translation. There is no escape.

Before I do, though, a word or two about what drew me to Ovid in the first place. I am so far from believing that the classical languages, especially as they appear in the works of their finest poets, are "irrelevant," "dead," or otherwise valueless to our age of internets and wi-fi and the Cloud, that I would gladly consign today's student and general reader (does he or she still exist?) to a lifelong study of Virgil, Horace, and Ovid—even if it meant sacrificing the ability to outgame one's peers at World of Warcraft.

For everything that really matters to us mattered to them. Their poems are imbued with human passion, suffering, wonder, and excitement, and they constitute a priceless record of how the very finest literary artists of the past dealt with the most intensely human subjects. They are part of a continuing conversation, and a precious heritage of the best-considered artistry of those who are every bit as much a part of us as we are of those to follow us. They are the ultimate riposte to a degrading and debilitating "presentism."

And of these artists, perhaps none is more capacious, free-roaming, exuberant, and passionately committed to every aspect of verse as a means of human exploration (and intellectual and aesthetic pleasure) than Ovid. His *Amores* and *Ars Amatoria* are witty, sophisticated, ironic, and a constant delight, treating a subject we can all understand as perpetually human. When love and lust disappear from the world, perhaps these poems may be allowed to wither and die. Till then, however . . .

When I began work on *Amores* and the *Ars Amatoria* at the turn of the century, I made sure to equip myself with Lewis and Short's *A Latin Dictionary* (to me, the finest, most scholarly, most helpful Latin dictionary ever) and Traupman's *New College Latin & English Dictionary*, with its blessedly time-saving set of paradigms positioned in the first few pages—never too soon to be reminded of one's high school and college drills in declension and conjugation.

I next availed myself of seven other translations of both works and consulted them often (a list appears at the end of this Preface). Much can be learned from the disagreements among translators (probably a great deal more than from their consonance), and I tried to consider as many possibilities as I could for word choice, syntactical probability, and (if the phrase has any meaning) plain prose sense. What translator doesn't? Where conflict proved intractable, I opted for the meaning that seemed to fit best with the tone and mood of the immediate lexical environment. Context and common sense would rule.

There followed a prose paraphrase (I believe Dryden[3] was right in saying that this is, finally, the only way to proceed, ignoring "imitation" and "metaphrase"). I simply could not envision myself as either Robert Lowell, whose *Imitations* represent work inspired by an original, or Christopher Logue, whose *War Music* and other volumes completely reimagine Homeric material with a modern (and mordant) sensibility, nor could I see what was to be gained by becoming the twenty-first-century embodiment of A. E. Housman's haplessly comic, overliteral schoolboy. (A delightful modern version of *that* dilemma has been provided us by the fine classicist and poet Charles Martin[4] with his own school days attempt at Horace: "Yet you, Impervius, though not unknown to the unsanctified daughter of the Lacedaemonian, live neither meanly nor ostentatiously.") With this prose paraphrase before me, I began constructing iambic hexameter-pentameter couplets, trying to match Ovid as closely as possible, line-for-line. I settled on iambic meter for a number of reasons.

First, though honorable attempts at English dactylic hexameter for Virgilian epic have been made (Frederick Ahl's *Aeneid*, for example), I'm afraid the only real competence, if any, available to me as an English poet lay in the ancient, timeworn (and yes, some would say shopworn) iambic. It is the way I hear English verse (and often, English prose), and is the register in which my mental Muse is always "running"—a little like Pope, one might say, who claimed to "lisp in numbers." I am not at all averse to other meters in the English canon or in current poetry (who could *not* admire Byron's Assyrian coming down like the wolf on the fold?[5]), but I knew when I began these versions of Ovid that I would be writing iambic hexameter first lines, rounded off with pentameters.

Still, the vexed question of *rhyme*: what possible defense could I adduce for rhymed couplets, when classical Latin almost never uses the device? (The very few instances in the work of Virgil and Ovid and Catullus only serve to prove the main point.) Latin poets make their music out of long and short syllables (their meters are *quantitative*), out of assonance and consonance and alliteration, and the wonderful play of broad, open vowels against short, forward ones, in patterns of contrast and balance and antithesis. Music *is* there.

The question that faced me was, could I possibly duplicate it? Well, Shakespeare could, and other practitioners of rich and sensuous blank verse (Wordsworth, Milton, Wallace Stevens), but it would have been a daunting task, far beyond my capabilities. I settled for the obvious expedient: my versions of Ovid would try for the snap and elegant closure of a finished-off, rhymed couplet, with whatever attendant graces could be added by my attempts at alliteration and assonance and syntactical play, as the opportunities presented themselves. And of course, I could always comfort myself with the observation that centuries of English poets have created their versions of classical poets in rhyme. To the objection that Dryden makes Virgil sound like Dryden and Pope makes Homer sound like Pope, I can only reply, "Would that I could enter such exalted company!" I fully realize that Latin scholars will object, and yes, there have indeed been attempts at exact, unrhymed, accentual-syllabic-equivalent translations of Latin's quantitative meters. But the results have never given me much pleasure *as poetry*, and if poems are not to be translated into other poems, why bother at all? It is the totality of the poem—its sounds and syntax and tones, as well as its sense—that define it, and not *just* the sense. The very last thing I wanted was for readers unfamiliar with Ovid to finish my translations and ask, "So what's the fuss? I thought Ovid was supposed to be a *poet*." Readers still skeptical are invited to peruse these exact, unrhymed versions and judge of their aesthetic qualities.

Finally, some minor notes on my technical practice. In order to make my task easier, I have, in a number of instances, played fast and loose with certain features of metrical, rhymed English verse. I have, for example, availed myself, wherever necessary, of the convention of the floating possessive: sometimes my meter requires *Venus'* and sometimes *Venus's* son. Many of my lines are "headless," by which I simply mean that the first syllable in a line otherwise iambic has been omitted. I have substituted an occasional trochaic first foot for an iambic, leading to what the ancients called a choriamb. I have also substituted an occasional trochee or spondee for an iambic foot at different positions in the metrical line. Readers who have been hearing my otherwise fairly regular meters in their heads will possibly notice these substitutions, but I doubt they will be overly discomfited by them.

In the matter of rhymes, I have on a very few occasions settled for what I hope are acceptably close near-rhymes or off-rhymes. The reader is assured that I did so only because I could find no alternative. (Some cruxes are never resolved.) So-called feminine end-rhymes occasionally appear (di-syllabic rhymes such as "making" and "taking"), followed at the start of new lines by an iamb or trochee, as the sense of the line seemed to require.

And with all these constraints in mind, I have tried to bring to the reader an English Ovid dealing with love in all its permutations.

Some translations of Ovid consulted:
Ovid: The Art of Love, trans. James Michie
Ovid's Amores, trans. Guy Lee
Ovid: The Art of Love, trans. Rolfe Humphries
Ovid: The Love Poems, trans. A. D. Melville
Ovid: The Erotic Poems, trans. Peter Green
Ovid: The Art of Love and Other Poems, trans. J. H. Mozley
Ovid in English, ed. Christopher Martin

Amores

Epigram of the Poet Himself

Five little books of Naso's once, now we are three—
    The way the author wished his work to be.
So even if you don't enjoy as you read on,
    That reading should hurt less—with two books gone.

BOOK I

I.1

Prepared for war, I set the weapon of my pen
 To paper, matching meter, arms, and men
In six feet equal to the task. Then Cupid snatched
 A foot away, laughing at lines mis-matched.
I asked him who had made *him* Master of My Song: 5
 "Wild little boy, we poets all belong
To the Muses. You don't see Venus bear the shield
 Minerva wears, or blonde Minerva wield
The lover's torch. And who would want the woods to yield
 To Ceres, or Diana rule the field?   10
Is long-haired Phoebus meant to march on pike parade
 While Mars shows how the Aonian lyre's played?
Your power, boy, runs every single thing in sight,
 So why this all-devouring appetite
For more? Or must your writ run clear to Helicon   15
 And up each string Apollo plays upon?
My first, fierce line: how well that virgin verse once served me—
 Until the simpering second one unnerved me!
But I don't have the matter for those lighter stresses—
 No girl—or boy—with long and comely tresses."   20
Then I was done, and Cupid fetched an arrow fletched
 For me (since on its shaft my name was etched).
He bent that reflex bow of his against one knee,

Saying what burden he had meant for me:
　　"Receive this barb, my bard." Well, Cupid is the best　　　　25
　　　　Of archers, so that bolt burns in my breast,
While six feet rise and five pronounce my clear decline
　　　　In elegiacs. Farewell, epic line.
And bind your golden locks with myrtle from the sea,
　　　　Eleven-footed Muse of Elegy.　　　　　　　　　　30

I.2

Because it's stone, I ask who's made my bed this way:
　　　　Sweet sleep slips off, and sweat-soaked sheets won't stay.
All night I cannot sleep at all, but toss and turn
　　　　Until my bones ache and my muscles burn.
I think I'd know if racking Love tormented me—　　　　5
　　　　Unless he hid his arts in secrecy.
That must be it. He's let it fly, his sneaky dart,
　　　　And I'm so weak, he twists it in my heart.
Should I give in—and up? Or fight—and feed the fire?
　　　　Surrender, or he'll pile the pyre higher!　　　　10
(I've seen what happens when you flourish one small brand:
　　　　Flame leaps. But don't? It dies out in your hand.)
They whip an ox that fights the yoke and will not pull,
　　　　But ploughing's painless for a docile bull.
The fiercest stallion breaks his mouth on iron bits;　　　　15
　　　　The broken filly feels a curb that fits.
So Love will crush that bridling enemy who braves
　　　　Him—crush him harder than surrendering slaves.
And Cupid, look: I'm one! Your newest prize says yes,
　　　　And puts his hands up. See how I profess　　　　20
Your creed? Your word is law; there is no war. I plead

For peace, so where's the glory in a deed
Like conquering an unarmed man? No, braid your hair
    With myrtle, hitch your mother's pigeon pair
To Vulcan's chariot, and in that war car, steer   25
    Those doves, as crowds cry out their love and cheer.
And youth that you lead on, those captive girls and boys,
    Will make a mighty triumph of your toys.
Myself, your latest spoil, will wear a wound that's fresh,
    Bearing as mind-forged chains what binds the flesh.   30
Good Sense and Shame, their hands bound back by cuff and clamp,
    Trudge on with everyone not in Love's camp.
The crowd that cries your triumph "Io!" cries from fear,
    Hands high. Their one great throat gives out that cheer.
Then Frenzy and Delusion follow in your train   35
    Forever, and caresses made in vain.
These are your forces that defeat all human foes;
    Sans them, you're just a boy without his clothes.
Oh, how your mother high above will clap, and shower
    Your head with roses in your finest hour!   40
You'll shine like gold, with jeweled wings, gems in your hair.
    Your golden self will dazzle all the air.
And we who know you well, know you will leave wound-free
    Few souls you fire with your ardency.
Boy Archer, all your arrows are their own. Blind seer,   45
    They scorch and singe whatever they come near,
As if you were great Bacchus on the Ganges' shore,
    Whose tigers had been tamed—like doves—for war.
So spare me as a victim in your triumph's train,
    And save your breath to blast some other swain.   50
Extend the kindness cousin Caesar's smiles exude:
    His arms reach out to each new land subdued.

I.3

Love, give me justice. Make my heart's thief love me, *or. . .*
  Make her the one I'll live forever for.
No, that's too much to ask. Just let her let me love,
  And hear my prayers, O Venus up above.
Accept me for a man who'll be your lifelong servant;   5
  Take one who in your faith will be observant
Despite the fact my family name's not old or fine,
  And though it's just a knight who "wrote" our line.
Perhaps our family can count its fields and ploughs,
  And parsed-out pennies are all it allows   10
Me. Phoebus, though, and Bacchus, and the Muses, and
  Amor, deliver me into your hand.
I'll offer you the greatest trust, love free from stain,
  And proper modesty—all clean and plain.
I am no ladies' man who jumps from horse to horse,   15
  Some circus rider, but will stay the course
Spun out by Clotho through the years—their whole, long thread—
  And die with you beside me at my bed.
You only need to give yourself to be my theme
  To see that what I write's worth your esteem.   20
Recall those other famous women: she who turned
  Bovine; and one a swan left not quite spurned;
That girl who went to sea with what just seemed a bull
  (Her virgin hands held horns to push and pull)?
Oh, we'll be sung that way throughout the world forever—   25
Two names that earth and time will never sever.

I.4

Your husband's coming to our feast? That same repast
     I'm praying will turn out to be his last?
So I must see my darling like some common guest;
     Watch any banquet hanger-on caressed.
Shall someone else, some man, grow warmer in my place,   5
     Arms round your neck in casual embrace?
No wonder that the wedding of Atrax's daughter
     Drew both those men *and* half-men to the slaughter!
But not for me some Centaur's home; my members mean
     To have you like a man's. That's plainly seen.   10
So memorize what you must do (don't give the South
     Wind or the East these words fresh from my mouth):
Arrive before him. As to why, I cannot say:
     What could we do? Come early anyway.
Then when he lies down on the couch, go modestly,   15
     But brush against my foot in secrecy.
And watch my subtle looks, my eyes, communicate;
     Catch all my hints . . . and then reciprocate.
Arch words that make no sound will speak from silent brows.
     Observe my hands; in wine, they'll trace my vows.   20
When you are thinking of our hungry, errant hands,
     Finger your cheeks as if with blushing brands.
Or if you're harboring against me some complaint,
     Tug gently on your earlobe as a feint.
My darling, when I speak and you approve the sound,   25
     Then smile . . . and twirl one of your rings around.
Hands down like those in prayer, palm the banquet table . . .
     To wish him all the curses you are able.
The wine he stirs for you, let your husband drink—take heed!

Then whisper your choice to the ganymede.   30
The cup that's been refilled, I'll take and drink from first,
    Sipping from where your lips have quenched their thirst.
If he should offer you some dainty that he's tasted,
    Refuse your husband's food; let it be wasted.
Don't let him throw his arms around your slender shoulder   35
    Or draw you to that chest hard as a boulder.
Make sure his nimble fingers never find your breast.
    Don't let him kiss you—this above the rest!
Just let his lips touch yours and I'll stand up and swear
    They're mine, revealing my love then and there.   40
But these are open torts; the robe you wear, my dear,
    Hides things that fill me with a cold, blind fear.
Don't let your thigh touch his; don't let his brush your leg.
    Your soft foot touch his rough one? No, I beg!
I fear so much because I've boldly done it, too.   45
    See how my own acts act like rack and screw,
So often have we two too fast made sweetest haste,
    Beneath unfastened robes, to touch and taste.
Do as I say, not as we do: lest someone think
    So, let your tell-tale cloak slip off and slink.   50
Keep urging him to drink, not kiss. There, draw the line.
    And while he drinks, in secret add more wine.
Then when he's been put down in just this vinous sleep,
    Pure chance will show the counsel we're to keep.
When you get up to go and everybody rises,   55
    Get thronged about—and wait for my surprises.
(You'll find me in that crowd, or else be found by me:
    Touch any part of me you cannot see.)
But what's the use? All this is only good for hours,
    Then night will ban me from you with its powers.   60

At night your husband locks you in, and I, half gone
    In grief, will stand outside your door till dawn.
Cold iron door! That man will kiss—and rub and paw!
    With you, what's love with me, with him is law.
But give against your will—you can—as if coerced.   65
    Show him a deaf, dumb Venus at her worst.
Give him no pleasure, if my words have any weight;
    If not, please don't be pleased at any rate.
But come what may, tomorrow, say in constancy
    You gave him nothing you have given me.   70

I.5

One summer afternoon, the sultry day half gone,
    I sought my bed to spread my limbs upon,
With half my window opened wide and half shut tight,
    Admitting just the softest woodland light—
The faintest gloaming as lord Phoebus starts to go,   5
    Or night gives way before the dawn's faint glow.
(They were the rays in which shy virgins try to hide,
    In hopes timidity won't yield to pride.)
Then came Corinna in her tunic cinched and sheer;
    Her fair neck felt her parted hair fall clear.   10
They say Semiramis went to her bed like this,
    And Lais, who for countless men meant bliss.
I snatched that tunic from her, and it caused no harm,
    But still she fought me for it in alarm.
She fought like one who fought a battle not to win,   15
    But struggled weakly, only to give in.
And as she stood, a sweet disorder in her dress,
    Her body showed no fault; my eyes said yes.

Such arms I saw and touched—soft, lean and strong, yet fine!
  Her round breasts fit two hands—and they were mine!   20
How smooth the rest of her, her legs so soft and lean,
  Her waist and thigh as fair as I have seen.
But why describe each charm when every charm I saw
  Was lovely, nude? We hugged; I filled with awe.
Who doesn't know what's next? Fatigued, we stopped to rest   25
  So I might pray, "Make all mid-days so blessed"

I.6

You there! Yes, you—my darling's doorman-porter-Janus:
  Swing back those hinges crying out "Unchain us!"
I don't ask much—just leave the door ajar a crack
  So I can slip in sideways—and get back.
There's been so much hard love of late that now, I'm thin   5
  Enough and light enough to wriggle in.
And that's what's taught me how to tip-toe past the guard:
  Love's suffering. Love makes footsteps soft, not hard.
There was a time when every phantom caused me fright;
  I was amazed that men went out at night.   10
Then Cupid, with his tender mother, laughed at me.
  He whispered, "You'll get brave; just wait and see."
And presto! Love walked in. Now, flighty nighttime spirit,
  Or knife that threatens doom, I just don't fear it.
Instead, it's *you* I fear, and you're the one I flatter,   15
  Who threatens thunderous ruin and can batter
My heart. Throw back the bolt so you can see me better.
  My tears have drenched the door; it can't be wetter.
You know I carried pleas to her! (You stood there stripped
  And trembling, slave, and ready to be whipped.)   20

Now that same grace I won for you, that once prevailed—
    Ingratitude!—for me has only failed.
Grant me this favor and you'll get your wish—and more;
    The midnight hours fly; unbar the door.
Cast off the bar and you will lose your chains, I say,   25
    Never to be a slave for one more day!
But you won't hear my bootless prayers, you porter cast
    In iron, while the oaken door stands fast.
Remember: towns besieged are towns that bar the door;
    So porter, why fear me? We're not at war.   30
If that's *my* lot, think how real foes would suffer more!
    The midnight hours fly; unbar the door.
I've come with no platoon of pikes and swords to fear.
    In fact, I'd be alone if Love weren't here,
And savage Love's a god I can't shake off; I'd stand   35
    A better chance of cutting off my hand.
So Love, you see, attends me—and a modest wine
    That roils this head crowned with a scent-soaked vine.
Who'd fear such arms? They're only trifles—nothing more;
    The midnight hours fly; unbar the door.   40
Stubborn? Or is it sleep—sleep curse your heart!—that steers
    My love-words windward from your mulish ears?
Oh, I remember when I first eluded you;
    You watched the stars till twelve, alert and true.
Perhaps some sweetheart sleeps beside you now? If so,   45
    Your lot's a better one than mine, you know.
I'd even welcome shackles and complain no more.
    The midnight hours fly; unbar the door.
Am I deceived, or did the door post shake and groan
    As hinges turned and made an awful moan?   50
I *am* deceived! The wind just knocked the door ajar,

Then took my hopes and scattered them afar.
    But Boreas, young Orithyia once was yours;
        Just think of her—and blast these stone-deaf doors.
The still town's dew collects; soon night will be no more.   55
        The midnight hours fly; unbar the door.
Now if you don't, with torch and crowbar, I will smash
        Your haughty house and turn it into ash.
Night, Love, and Wine all counsel lack of self-restraint:
        Night knows no shame and Love and Wine no taint   60
Of fear. But every prayer and threat I've tried has failed
        To move a man so thick and tightly nailed.
And oh, my darling's guard: to think that you prevailed,
        Who's better fit to watch and ward the jailed!
Already frosty Lucifer begins to roll;   65
        The cock cries "Wake and work!" to every soul.
But you, you wretched garland snatched from off my head,
        Lie all night long on stone blocks that are dead.
You'll be the witness in the morning so she'll know
        I spent this faithful, awful night in woe.   70
And you, you slave: good-bye, and here's your Parthian prize:
        You held, indifferent to this lover's cries.
Farewell to rigid threshold, post, and beam as well;
        You are this servant's slaves, and never fell.

I.7

If anyone here is my friend, then clamp my wrists
        With fetters earned, while frenzy still persists.
For with my fists, my madness beat my mistress dear;
        It was those blows that brought these tears, I fear.
When it was happening, I could have hit my own   5

Parents, or whipped a god upon his throne!
Well, didn't Ajax of the Seven Folds of Shield
    Destroy Greek flocks and run mad through the field?
And didn't Agamemnon's son avenge him ill,
    When he attacked the gods he sought to kill?   10
So surely I could tear my darling's hair and mangle
    It? Yet it lay so lovely in a tangle.
In her own way, she glowed like Atalanta when
    With windblown hair she hunted through the glen.
And Ariadne, too, who wept when the headstrong   15
    South wind blew Theseus and his sails headlong.
Cassandra, too (but she wore headbands)—she who threw
    Herself upon Minerva's mercy. Who
Then failed to call me mad barbarian? My dear
    One stood in silence, trembling in her fear.   20
Her bloodied face reproached me as she held her peace,
    Though still accusing (tears found their release).
And I had sooner see my arm fall off than see
    Her cry—yes, live without that part of me.
Assaulting her, I've made foul shame my just desert,   25
    Overpowering her to my own hurt.
So what have I to do with these, a felon's hands?
    Come shackle them, as justice now demands.
If I had struck the lowest of the lowly, I'd
    Be whipped; strike her and law's still on my side?   30
Or think of Tydeus' son, who left the worst
    Example: wound a goddess? He's the first,
Then I! But I am worse, who've injured her—the one
    I love; he fought a foe, Tydeus' son.
Now go prepare your heady victory parade,   35
    Laurel your hair, and count the prayers you've made

To Jove. Let all the crazed crowd cry and cheer and wave.
    They'll shout, "This brute has made a girl his slave,
We see!" Then lead her captive, sad, with hair unloosed,
    All white, except for cheeks blood-red and bruised.   40
Better by far my pressing lips had left their mark,
    With teeth that had caressed her neck with stark
Imprints. But in the end, if madness meant to drive
    Me, blind rage hunting down its man alive,
Why didn't I just shout at her, that timid girl?   45
    Instead . . . the menaces I thought to hurl!
Why not have torn her fragile dress from neck to waist?
    At least her girdle would have kept her chaste.
But no—I had to rake her temples, rip her hair,
    And blood a lady's cheeks I tried to tear.   50
Dumbfounded, there she stood, her pale face drained and drawn,
    Whiter than Parian marble blocks fresh-sawn.
I saw her body shake, heir to a thousand shocks,
    The way the winds blow poplars' leafy locks,
And lenient Zephyr plays his breath on slender canes,   55
    Or tepid Notus combs blue wavy manes.
Then tears that she had dammed flowed down her face at last,
    Like runneling piles of snow soon melting fast.
And that's the moment when I knew what I had done—
    Hot tears. My blood ran cold as blood can run.   60
That's when I would have flung myself down at her feet
    Even if three times she should flail and beat
My ugly hands away. O darling, grant me grace . . .
    And rake *your* outraged nails across *my* face.
Don't spare my eyes or hair; the weakest hand gains might   65
    In righteous anger. Hide my crime from sight—
At least its vile red signs of my abject disgrace:
    Re-dress your locks . . . and comb them back in place.

I.8

There is a madam—let who'll listen come to learn—
    Called Dipsas Crone: a name she drank to earn,
It suits her; sober is a thing she hasn't been
    Since Memnon's mother—whom she's never seen.
But Dipsas knows Aeaean chants and magic's force   5
    So well, she makes streams flow back to their source.
She knows her magic threads; what poisons to prepare
    From herbs; the power of the secreting mare
At estrus. Yes, when Dipsas wants, the clouds appear;
    She speaks? Blue firmament shines free and clear.   10
And if you could believe it, I have seen stars ooze
    With blood, and Luna's face a purple bruise.
I'm almost sure she flies through night's infernal glooms,
    Her hag-like body thatched about with plumes.
At least I'm almost sure as Rumor. Two-eyed lightning   15
    Streaks from her pupils make her doubly frightening,
Who calls her ancient ancestors from hoary tombs
    And splits the solid earth with spells and dooms.
Though she's prepared to do our modest bond great harm,
    Her poisoned tongue is not without its charm.   20
I know. By chance I heard my darling being bidden
    This way (behind two doors where I lay hidden):
"My light, were you aware that yesterday, a well-
    Off fellow saw your face? Oh, how he fell!
Why not? Your looks are finer than the rest, bar none.   25
    But oh, what charming clothes can you put on?
Too bad, my dear, you're not as fortunate as fair;
    If you were rich, I wouldn't have a care.
Leaving you poor, the star of Mars goes retrograde,
    As Venus reigns and Mars begins to fade.   30

Just see how her ascendance means the best for you!
    There's nothing that this rich man wouldn't do.
A man whose face, with yours—and you—will nicely pair.
    If he weren't buying, girls would want a share
Of him." My darling blushed. "True blushing's nice on faces,   35
    But phony blushes profit in more cases.
Demurely scan his gifts with oh-so-modest eyes,
    And rate him—by their quantity and size.
Maybe plain Sabine women, less than fair and gracious,
    Stayed true to one man in the reign of Tatius,   40
But Mars is off to try men's souls; while he's away,
    Venus rules Rome so gorgeous girls can play.
The only girl who's chaste is one who's still unasked;
    If not a farm girl, she herself has asked!
Examine, too, that woman's face that furrows plough;   45
    She may hide devilish sins behind that brow.
Penelope tried young men with her husband's bow
    Of horn, testing the strength they strove to show.
My dear, time slips away so silently, unseen,
    Like streams that race to be Heraclitean.   50
Fair bronze stays bright with use; fine clothes will beg for wear.
    A house abandoned dies in disrepair.
So beauty, too, declines if you do not admit
    At least three rich young men to work on it.
(Besides, you'll rake in more good booty you can keep.)   55
    For wolves to feast, it takes a flock of sheep.
And think: poor poets only give you more poor verses,
    Thousands of which will never fill our purses.
Even Apollo, poet-god, wears golden cloaks
    To match the golden lyre's strings he strokes.   60
No, let rich suitors mean far more than Homer could;

Giving requires practice to be good.
And don't despise a slave that's recently redeemed:
    Chalked feet were never the stigma they seemed.
Don't be misled by portraits hanging in the hall;   65
    Remove your 'sires,' poor lovers, one and all!
Adonises who think they needn't pay should first
    Grace you with loot their lovers have disbursed.
Spreading your net, be subtle as to price, so he
    Won't flee. Then when he's trapped, set your own fee.   70
Faking true love's all right, letting him think you care,
    But don't let 'love' leave you a purse that's bare!
Tease him a hundred times; say that your temples ache.
    Say Isis gives you pause—a pause that's fake.
Later, bed him—enough to keep him coming back—   75
    Or too much *no* may make his love go slack.
Slam shut your door on tears, but always welcome gold.
    Let new loves hear the pleading words of old,
And sometimes, make believe you're angry when you're wrong;
    He'll be believing you before too long.   80
Guilt-free then, over-doing anger's not advised,
    Since too much means you'll find yourself despised.
Like first-rate actresses, learn crying on demand;
    Use slave or mistress—anything at hand.
Don't be afraid to perjure, lying under oath.   85
    Venus approves of tricks; she's nothing loath.
Teach both your servant and your handmaid what is right
    For lovers' tribute in the sparkling night.
And have them ask for little gifts themselves. After awhile,
    From single straws will grow a giant pile.   90
Your mother, nurse, and sister, too, should pluck each man
    Till six hands grasp far more than six hands can.

Should pretexts and excuses ever peter out,
    A cake will make him ask, 'What's *that* about?'
Don't ever let him love secure, without a rival;   95
    No hurdles means love's doubtful of survival.
Let him see on your couch the ocular proof, the mess;
    And on your neck, love's purple tenderness.
Be more than quite particular he sees your many
    Gifts, but go buy some if you haven't any   100
(Try Via Sacra). Then, to get his last red cent,
    Demand he lend you sums you've no intent
Re-paying. Double-speak, and mask your thought, and flatter.
    Sweet honeycombs can hide pure poison matter.
Live by these words; I learned the hard way. Trust in me.   105
    And if no breeze should blow them out to sea,
You'll speak me well while I'm alive, and always pray
    My bones lie softly when I pass away."
Her words hung in the air still when my shadow moved,
    But strangler's hands (who would have disapproved?)   110
Barely refrained from clawing out her winey eyes
    And four last hairs; I longed to cicatrize
Her. Hag: God send you winter, homeless penury,
    And thirst that lasts for all eternity.

I.9

Yes, lover, soldier, Cupid—all are of one camp,
    My Atticus. They bear that single stamp
Of being just the age for Venus and for Mars
    (When either's old, that's awful, and it jars).
The spirit captains seek in soldiers is the same   5
    Young women want in those who play love's game:

Men who'll watch all night, and sleep on ground that's hard;
> At bedroom door, or camp, they'll stand their guard.
Soldiers march endless roads, it's true. Exile his dear,
> And lover-boy will search the last frontier,   10
Climbing the tallest mountain, fording streams swollen twice
> Their size, and wading snowdrifts laced with ice.
He won't use stars as an excuse why not to sail,
> Or big east winds, but rows on without fail.
And who but lovers will, like soldiers, stand the chill   15
> Of night, or sleet that bores down like a drill?
One man will spy on troops who carry swords and spears;
> The other eyes some rival that he fears.
This one besieges cities; that one just beseeches.
> One pounds on women's doors; the other breaches   20
City gates. To massacre an enemy
> Who sleeps unarmed can be good strategy.
Remember Thrace's butchered Rhesus and his men
> Whose horses will not heed their call again?
Surely when husbands sleep, Love's fierce exploits of war   25
> Take place, and weapons wave while thousands snore.
Always it's yearning lover's, soldier's, sacred duty
> To penetrate the lines that guard great booty—
Or beauty. And if Mars is fickle, Venus, too.
> The conquered rise, and mighty plans fall through.   30
So those who call Love lazy, rein your slander in!
> Love is for temperaments that burn to win.
Achilles raged, seeing Briseis hauled away,
> But Trojans failed to seize the Argive day.
It was Andromache who helmeted the head   35
> Of Hector; arming fast, he left her bed.
Field Marshal Agamemnon? He could only stare

At Maenad-mad Cassandra's windblown hair.
And Mars, ensnared by Vulcan, started in to moan.
  There was no joke in heaven better known.   40
So, what of me? I'd been a louche and lazy man,
  Soul-softened by his afternoon divan;
But now I love a beauty, and I'm rather nervous
  To sign up for a hitch in Cupid's service.
But if I do, just watch me on my night campaign.   45
  Enlist in love and *you* can start to train!

I.10

Like one the Phrygian ship tore from Eurotas' shores
  (That one who caused her dual husbands' wars);
Like Leda, whom the devious, disguised god conned,
  Plumed in bright white and loving as he swanned;
Like that Amymone who walked parched fields and pressed   5
  The full, cold urn to temples damply tressed:
That's how you were. For you, I feared the bull and eagle—
  Whatever form Love made of Jove the Regal.
Now all my fear is gone. My errant soul stands healed.
  Your beauty strikes; my eyes no longer yield.   10
Why have I changed, you ask? Because you make men buy
  You gifts. Now you displease, and that is why.
While you were guileless, you were loved, body and soul;
  Your heart now makes your beauty pay its toll.
Dear, Love's a little child; He can't be lewd   15
  Like us. He's innocent, despite he's nude.
So why should Cupid sell himself as prostitute?
  No garments mean no pockets for the loot!
Venus and Son are far from fit to join the fray;

Such peaceful gods deserve no soldier's pay. 20
It's those who stand for sale at one fixed price for all,
    Who grub for cash from bodies under thrall.
But even they still curse procurers for their greed.
    You freely choose; tarts do it out of need!
Model yourself on cattle. In their attributes, 25
    There is no reason; you're worse than those brutes.
No stallion rents the mare; no bull must somehow pay.
    What ewe has ever charged a ram to play?
No, only woman gloats at what she milks from man,
    Renting her charms for every "gift" she can, 30
Hard-selling what delights them both, what both desire,
    And as her pleasure rises, charges higher.
What should be rightly a delight to both is made
    A business deal that's fit for two-way trade.
So why should pleasure be my loss and yet your gain 35
    When man and woman make one pleasure twain?
Or think of perjury sold from the witness stand;
    A juror bought, or holding out his hand:
How vile to plead for lowly criminals with skill,
    In paid-for courts where justice comes to nil. 40
Shameful, to swell estates with ill-gotten returns.
    A tart's own cash your smashing beauty earns.
But graces freely granted—they should be admired.
    No thanks should go to love that's meanly hired.
Renting, the man who pays you pays once and for all, 45
    Which means he needn't heed your beck and call.
So, lovely women: set no price on your embrace;
    To price your love leads to a sordid place.
Gold Sabine cuffs: that's what Tarpeia haggled for;
    They crushed her under what their left arms wore. 50

Or one who had her womb son-slashed, from there to here,
  The lowly cause some gaudy lavaliere.
Still, there's no shame in winkling money from the rich,
  Who clearly have it, if your palm should itch.
I mean, go harvest grapevines; take their gravid fruit.   55
  Alcinous's fields should grant your suit
As well. Let paupers pay you with their faith and trust;
  They'll give their all. (Because they love, they must.)
And what of me? My verses dower each sweetheart;
  Whoso I list lives always in my art.   60
Rich cloaks will shred, and gems and gold will all decay,
  But in these lines you'll never fade away.
Dear, *giving's* not the rub, but that you'd have me *pay.*
  Stop asking and I'll pay you every day!

I.11

Napê, far more than any handmaid; far the best
  At training locks unruly and distressed;
And famous for your offices by dark of night;
  For sending lovers warning signals right,
And coaxing my Corinna from her doubt, to come;   5
  Napê, there is no task you've wavered from:
Take these furrowed tablets at dawn to her you serve,
  Careful that nothing makes you lag or swerve.
I know you have no flinty breast or iron heart,
  And you've been known to play a clever part.   10
I sense as well that *you* have felt blind Cupid's dart
  Yourself; so help your own cause with some art:
Should she inquire, just say I live on hope alone;
  In letter-graven wax, the rest is known.

Yet while I talk, time flies. So let her read at ease, 15
    But right away, good Napê, if you please.
And watch her eyes and forehead as she does; for though
    She's mute, my future's what her face will show.
Right after, have her write down every word she can;
    Huge margins are a thing I hate to scan, 20
For they should be pushed off the page by dense, tight lines
    That crowd the edge—love's thickly written signs.
Oh, why? *Why* make a pen cramp fingers till they're numb?
    Just have her write one word, and that word *come*!
I'd hurry then to crown these tablets all in bay, 25
    Votives on Venus' shrine, without delay.
Under, I'd write: "Naso gives these; their help was good,
    Though they were once the meanest maple wood."

I.12

Weep for my fate—tablets have come that sadly say,
    In lonely letters, "Darling, not today."
I should have known from Napê's omen: set to go,
    She stumbled, and the doorsill stubbed her toe!
Napê, next time you cross the threshold, keep in mind 5
    To lift your feet and leave the sill behind.
And you, you low-born, rotten tablet wood, get lost
    With all that bad-news wax I wish I'd tossed!
This wax was from some hemlock flower—wax sent by
    Those Corsican bees whose honey makes you die. 10
(I'd thought that you were wax dyed deep vermilion-red,
    But you were dyed in scarlet blood instead.)
Lie there, you less-than-useless wood, thrown in the road
    To be run over by some cart wheel's load.

Even the man who shaped you into useful wood,   15
    I'm certain worked with hands that were no good.
Your mother was a hanging tree: I hear necks break.
    You gave the executioner his stake
And lent the raucous horned owl shade in which to yowl.
    You raised the vulture and the screeching owl.   20
I must have been insane to send my love in these.
    Hard woods, soft words—and neither one could please.
These tablets were more fit for bail-bonds droning on
    In lawyers' mouths, until all hope was gone.
Better by far that they should lie in dull accounts,   25
    Where misers moan and groan at lost amounts.
So, tablets, you've been double-dealing, like your name;
    Your two wings meant no good—and no good came.
What should my rage pray for but that old age infect
    And eat and waste your wax with pale neglect?   30

I.13

From her old husband, Dawn comes blonde across the sea,
    With daybreak on her hoary axle-tree.
"Aurora, where so fast? Please wait! Let Memnon's rites
    Be done by ash-flown birds in yearly fights!
If there is ever joy, it's now, in her embrace,   5
    Where in her tender arms I've found my place.
And now indeed, when sleep is deep and air lies cool,
    Slim-throated birdsong is a crystal pool.
Now where so fast, bête noir of girls, of men the bane?
    With rosy hand, pull back the dewy rein.   10
Before you rise, the sailor sees his every star,
    So night-time navigation's best by far

The tired traveler knows you cannot be ignored;
    Dawn finds the soldier polishing his sword.
You're first to see the farmer wield his hoe and share,   15
    And call slow cattle to the yoke they wear.
You rob boys' sleep, then leave them in their tutors' hands;
    The teacher's whip enforces his commands.
You send too-sanguine souls to courts where they are heard—
    And lose their case through just a single word.   20
You make defense *and* plaintiff into two sad men
    Who every dawn must traipse to court again.
When women would prefer to work no more in wool,
    Dawn sets their quota to be met in full.
All this I could endure, but only loveless men   25
    Could bear girls rising when dawn's back again.
So many times I prayed that Night should not give way
    To you; that stars might see your face, yet stay.
I prayed so often winds would smash your axle and
    Your cloud-crashed team would plunge into the land.   30
O jealous Dawn, where do you rush? Your Ethiop son
    Was black; were your heart and your son's as one?
Too bad Tithonus isn't free to let us hear
    The gossip—heaven's juiciest, my dear.
You flee from age that sometime did you seek—foul age   35
    That drives you to those wheels that make him rage.
But if it were your Cephalus whom you embraced,
    You'd cry, 'Night's horses: slowly, slowly haste!'
Well, just because he's old, why should *I* have to suffer?
    I didn't make you marry that old duffer.   40
See all the sleep that Luna gives Endymion?
    And neither of you is the fairer one.
Was it not Jove himself, who keeping you at bay,

Made two nights out of one to have his way?"
My rant was done, and oh, she blushed at what I'd said.   45
    Still, at six sharp—not nine—the day broke red.

I.14

I used to tell you not to dye it, didn't I?
    But now your head has nothing left to dye.
If only you had let it grow: so rich and long,
    Your locks would still hang down—where they belong.
You would have feared to comb hair fine as that—so fine a   5
    Head, with strands like veils they wear in China.
A spider might have spun her threads that thin, that seem
    Like webs she wove from some deserted beam.
Your hair was neither black nor blonde, but mixed in hue,
    The way a bark-stripped cedar tree the dew   10
Has soaked in valleys far below some headlong side
    Of Ida looks—not light or darkly dyed.
And more than that, the hundred ways that you could train
    And braid your tresses never caused you pain.
No needle or comb's pickets ever tore your hair.   15
    Your lady's maid had nothing she should fear,
For I have seen her dress your tresses free from harm:
    No pin you wielded pricked her in the arm.
And when your hair lay all undone at dawn, you lay
    Upon your rich and purple couch halfway.   20
Yes, even then, as if upon the ground in Thrace,
    You seemed a Maenad in that verdant place.
Oh, down was rougher then than all your fine, soft hair—
    The hair you tried to torture, rack, and tear!
It bore up under that, though; gave itself to fire   25

And iron, forming ringlets forced to gyre.
I cried out then and called it crime: "A crime to burn
    Locks pretty on their own"—advice you'd spurn,
You iron heart! What violence! Don't scorch such hair.
    Your curls could teach those irons better care.   30
But now it's gone—hair Bacchus or Apollo might
    Have envied, wishing it were theirs! The sight
Of nude Dionê in that painting begged compare;
    She held up sea-soaked locks just like your hair.
And now, its forlorn fate is an excuse to moan,   35
    When, silly girl, the fault was all your own!
You're shocked to see yourself? You put your mirror down?
    Be strong! Forget that girl at which you frown.
No rival's potions hurt you; no Thessalian crone
    Employed her poison spring; the guilt's your own.   40
You lost your locks from no disease—please not that curse!—
    And no one's toxic talk was used—or worse.
No, all your loss you caused yourself by how you dyed
    With poison tints, by your own hand applied.
Shorn German women captives now shall make you whole;   45
    Giving their hair, the conquered play their role.
Then you will blush when anyone admires those waves,
    Crying, "I'm praised for what was bought from slaves!
Now some Sygambrian draws comments meant for me,
    When I was once a girl men fought to see."   50
Oh, woe is me! She cloaks her face and fights back tears.
    Her hands hide cheeks where blushing pink appears,
While in her lap the lost curls lie. She gives a sigh.
    A gift most undeserved. Oh me, oh my!
Compose yourself! Collect your thoughts! In only days,   55
    The locks you grow again will win you praise.

I.15

Gnawing Envy, it's "waste" of which I stand accused?
  You call my verse the work of wit misused,
And claim my youth disdains our Roman fathers' ways,
  Spurning to chase the soldier's dusty bays.
You say I won't learn verbose legalese, or sell   5
  Myself as thankless Forum mouthpiece? Well,
This "work" you want will die some day. The work I do
  Will live in deathless verse, the whole world through.
While Tenedos exists, so shall Maeonia's son.
  He'll live as long as Simois shall run.   10
Ascraean Hesiod lives so long as grapes make must
  And Ceres' wheat is scythed, or turns to dust.
The world will sing Callimachus; his verse assures
  His fame. When genius fails, fine craft endures.
Nothing will ever kill the plays of Sophocles.   15
  The sun and moon? Aratus outlives these.
While tricky slave, harsh sire, false bawd, and courtesan
  Endure, like them, Menander will go on.
Ennius in his art and Accius, tart of tongue,
  Are names the world will keep forever young.   20
What era won't know Varro or that ship the *Argo*
  (Aesonian heroes sought its golden cargo)?
Sublime Lucretius' poetry will pass away
  Only when Earth has seen its final day.
In pastoral and epic, Virgil will be read   25
  When Rome and worldwide Roman rule are dead.
Tibullus, while a torch and bow are Cupid's tools,
  Your numbers will be scanned in all the schools.
Gallus, from west to east! Great Gallus shall be known—

Gallus, famed with Lycoris as his own.   30
In fact, though time grinds down the stubborn plow and rock,
    Great lines go on, surviving every shock.
Before verse dies, let kings and all their pomp go down
    In Tagus' waters, there with gold to drown.
The crowd can worship what is crass; I'll drink that cup   35
    Of pure Castalian Phoebus has filled up,
And wear a myrtle wreath—that plant that fears the cold.
    Young lovers long will read me till they're old!
All envy feeds on what's alive; at death, it dies.
    Then fame's the thing that guards man's precious prize.   40
So when my body pays the flames its final debt,
    The best of me will go on living yet.

BOOK II

II.1

These lines are Naso's, too. From that Paelignian fen,
    I've come to shock you with my naughty pen.
These "useless" verses, Love demands, so . . . out of here!
    They're too much for the piously severe.
They should be read by girls who heat their lovers' blood,   5
    Or gawky boys, just coming to the flood.
I wish some man, heartstruck by arrows that struck me,
    Would get the point, and they would make him see.
Then he would have to ask, "How did this Naso find
    Out all I've suffered? Did he read my mind?"   10
I think back how I dared to write of heaven's wars
    And Gyas' hundred hands—great lines in scores.
I sang of Earth, its botched revenge, and Pelion piled
    On Ossa on Olympus, steep and wild.
I held the thunder-clouds, and Jove as well; I even   15
    Grasped the lightning for defending heaven.
But then I dropped him when my darling slammed her door,
    And Jove was not my burden anymore.
Forgive me, Jove! Your lightning was a one-day wonder;
    Her doors out-"bolted" yours with greater thunder.   20
For now, I'm armed with elegiac metaphors
    Whose charms have often softened hardened doors.
Well? Poetry has tractored blood-red Luna's horns

And turned Sol's horses round for longer morns.
What's versed has burst the viper's jaw and pulled its fang,   25
    Or sent streams back to springs from which they sprang.
Song has the strength to make doors open wide, and hard
    Oak bolts have yielded to a forceful bard.
What doth it profit me to sing Achilles' speed?
    Not one Atrides ever met my need.   30
What can Ulysses do, ten years at war, ten gone?
    Or Hector, by Haemonian horses drawn?
No. Tender girls whom poets praise for lips and eyes
    And hair will vie to be some poet's prize.
The gifts gods give! Great epic heroes' names, good-bye!   35
    Your graces were not meant for such as I.
Girls, turn your lovely faces here; I sing to you
    The songs that rosy Love has told me to!

II.2

Bagoas, you entrusted with your mistress' care:
    I have a few choice words I'd like to share.
Just yesterday I saw her stroll the colonnade
    Where Danaus's carved girls haunt the shade.
I saw; she pleased. I said "I want you" in a note.   5
    In shaky script, "I can't," is all she wrote.
I sent back, "*Why?*" But her note, not to be out-quicked,
    Shot back, "The watch he keeps is far too strict."
Now if you're wise, you'll trust me; win yourself a friend—
    And not someone who wants your life to end!   10
Her husband's less than wise as well, to guard what couldn't
    Be "lost"—her honor—even if he wouldn't.
But let his love infatuate him; let him call

Her chaste who's known so many . . . pleasing all.
Meanwhile, give her some furtive freedom; let her play,   15
    And in return, she'll set you free some day.
Conspire with her and she'll be yours in servitude.
    But fake it if you fear you can't collude.
She'll read my note in private—if "her mother" sent it,
    Then know this stranger's note, and that I meant it.   20
Perhaps a visit to a friend she swore was sick?
    Let her go see! That ought to do the trick.
If she's not back by midnight, don't wait up; just rest.
    Then snore away, your head drooped on your chest.
One temple's safe—that's Isis'—Isis cloaked in linen.   25
    And theatres have not let *that* much sin in.
Be silent and your palms can grow much greasier;
    I can't think what could be much easier.
A man like that could run the house: no whip, no word.
    And at his feet? The stupid servant-herd.   30
Don't let her husband guess just why; make up some lies.
    Whatever Mistress wants, her husband buys.
I mean, he *tries* to scowl and knit that manly brow,
    But ends up doing what she wants—and now.
Sometimes, a phony scolding lends a certain cover,   35
    Where you're "the executioner" of her.
Make straw-man accusations of her; if you do,
    Then no one will believe a charge that's true.
That way, your loot will always grow. And if you save,
    Who knows! Some day, you may not be a slave!   40
You know informers earn a set of chains for pay,
    And dungeons hold the faithless who betray.
Think Tantalus: he bends to drink; the pool recedes.
    His once loose tongue wants fruit, but never feeds.

Or Argus, watching Io—over-close. He died   45
    Too soon; now she's a goddess Jove enskied.
I've seen slaves wearing shackles on their livid shins
    Because they made men face their spouse's sins.
Those chains were less than what was earned. Talk ruins two:
    The husband grieves; her honor is all through.   50
Trust me: the truth will kill a blindly-loving man.
    Be kind; tell him as little as you can.
A lukewarm man ignores the tales poured in his ear;
    A loving man hates what you make him hear.
Besides, to prove her guilty isn't such a cinch . . .   55
    When judge and girl are kissing in a clinch.
Sometimes men credit girls despite their very eyes;
    Doubting their sight, they soothe themselves with lies.
A husband sees her tears and starts in wailing, too:
    "This *tattler*! Oh, the *things* I mean to do!"   60
Why fight a losing battle! You'll just get the strap,
    While Missus sits there in the judge's lap.
Bagoas, this is not a crime: we've drawn no sword,
    Nor mixed no poison for your lady's lord.
I ask you: help us safely love. Now could there be   65
    An easier request or simpler plea?

II.3

Poor me, that *you* should guard her. Neither girl nor man,
    You cannot know the joyous love *we* can.
Who first made eunuchs out of boys deserved the same
    As all those striplings that he thought to maim.
Oh, listening to our prayers would surely make you melt—   5
    If passion were a thing you'd ever felt.

But you weren't born for chargers or for force of arms,
    And hurling spears is *not* one of your charms.
(Let men be tough; you just weren't made for manly ways.)
    No, it's your mistress' banner you should raise.   10
If you would thrive, go tell her all the good you've done.
    Without her help, you'd end up all alone.
She's got the face and figure—just the age to play.
    Neglect them and those charms will waste away.
She could have come to me, in spite of just how strict   15
    You are; when two collude, you can be tricked.
Still, begging you's a better policy, no doubt.
    But quick!—your chance to help is running out.

II.4

I won't defend my faulty morals. Wouldn't dare.
    And wouldn't lie to make what's foul seem fair.
No, I confess—for all the good it does—my sins
    (My half-crazed soul is where such crime begins).
I hate myself, and what I can't *not* be, I hate.   5
    Oh, Atlas-like, I long to drop my fate.
Too weak to rule myself, all self-restraint now lost,
    I ride the waves, a toy ship turned and tossed.
There is no one fixed type that sets my heart aflame;
    A hundred causes make me play The Game.   10
If she's so modest she can't look me in the face,
    I burn, and till she captures me, I chase.
But if she's brash, I'm overjoyed she's not some hick;
    That means she won't just lie there like a stick.
If she seems Sabine-cold and plays the matron, then   15
    I'm sure she's lying and would yield to men.
A learned girl? She's mistress of the choicest arts.

Unlettered? Dull? Plain minds mean simple hearts.
Suppose "Callimachus is crude" compared to me.
    Oh, joy! Love thrives on reciprocity.   20
But if some other girl "despises" all I write,
    I take her in my arms and hug her tight.
A light step? How I love her! Someone's stiff? She'll melt
    As soon as this man's softening touch is felt.
Because one girl can sing and trill with ease, I long   25
    To kiss her in the middle of her song.
Another plucks the plangent strings with flitting thumb?
    That's it! Her dexterous hand must strike me dumb.
Some beauty dances—arms like willows, hips like snakes—
    Then what a stir her gentle movement makes.   30
Say nothing of the fact no charmer can escape us;
    Hippolytus in my shoes turns Priapus!
My tall girl, fit for one of the *Heroides*,
    Your noble length could fill this couch with ease.
My sweet petite, you're fine; I love you both—I do!   35
    Legs long *and* short? I love the both of you.
Say this one's not so chic; I think what clothes could add.
    Say that one is; her charms just can't look bad.
Pale women win me; blondes, I'm ready for the catching.
    But even dusky Venuses are fetching.   40
If raven ringlets runnel down some snow-white back,
    I've looked on Leda—and her hair was black.
If yellow locks, Aurora wore a head of gold
    (My love can fit the oldest stories told).
Young ones tempt me, but older women tempt my arms.   45
    One's worthier; the other boasts true charms.
To sum up: every girl in Rome who's thought a gem—
    My catholic taste desires all of them.

II.5

No love should mean so much—fly, quivered Cupid, fly!—
     That I should pray so many times to die.
I made so many prayers, each caused by some affair.
     Your mother bore you for my pure despair!
No rubbed-out tablet told me plainly all you did;   5
     No sneaky gift revealed the things you hid.
Too bad I have so strong a case; too bad for sure—
     To win it would be too much to endure.
Lucky the man defending her who gets to hear,
     "You must believe I didn't do it, dear."   10
(They're iron prosecutors, loving their own pain,
     Who'd "win" by seeing the defendant slain.)
But I was sober when you thought I slept. I saw,
     Through bottles, how you broke our lovers' law.
I saw your eyebrows quivering from the words you said;   15
     You spoke too much when you would nod your head.
Your eyes were talking, too, and fingers traced—in wine,
     With every letter—what was his, not mine.
I saw your talk said things I wasn't meant to see
     In loaded words charged with duplicity.   20
Leaving the tables then, the crowd went stumbling out.
     A boy or two slept deep amid that rout,
And that's when you and he began to grope and kiss
     (The tongues you forked weren't all that hard to miss).
They weren't the kind a sister gives her proper brother,   25
     But rather, her significantly other.
Could Phoebus kiss his sister this way? No, it jars.
     But Venus must have kissed this way with Mars.
"Where are you scattering my joys? What's this you do?

I'm going to assert my rights; with you,   30
They're common to me, and with me, to you," I shout.
    "Third parties have no claim, beyond a doubt."
That's what I said, and frenzy made me say a lot.
    But then . . . that blood-red look she got!
She colored up like Dawn, fresh out of bed—   35
    The face a (lucky) groom sees, newly-wed.
She pinked like lilies tinctured by a scarlet rose,
    Or Autumn's moon, bewitched and in her throes.
She looked like Lydian ivory women have to dye
    To keep from yellowing as time goes by.   40
Well, one of these, or something close, describes her face
    Far at its best when she was in disgrace.
She hung her head, and oddly, hanging most became her;
    Sorrow and beauty joined there just to shame her.
The way she was—and she was fine—I meant to tear   45
    Her cheeks to shreds and rip that long, chic hair.
But when I saw her face, I dropped my arms. They fell
    Down at my sides, for she was armed as well.
Enraged before, I begged her now to kiss me, good
    And hard and long—the longest that she could.   50
She smiled and did her best, and God, her best could jolt
    Great Jove and make him drop his thunderbolt.
And yet . . . others had it so good; *they* got this kind
    Of kiss, and that drives me out of my mind.
For this was better than I'd taught her how to do . . .   55
    Which makes it clear she'd learned a trick or two.
Her kissing was *too* good, and that was just too bad,
    For it was skilled—the schooling that she'd had.
It isn't just her wayward tongue that has me irked,
    And yet I'm grieved at how it's overworked.   60

She could have learned this nowhere but in bed. I say
  Her teacher truly earned exquisite pay.

II.6

Her parrot, feathered mime from India, has died.
  Come crowd his grave, birds; come from far and wide,
Devoted fliers. Beat your breasts with wings. Come, bands
  Of birds, and scar your cheeks with crooked hands.
As mourners rip their hair, let torn plumes show regrets   5
  And kind hearts' songs stand in for your cornets.
Now, Philomel, if you lament King Tereus' crime,
  Leave off; that long lament has had its time.
Turn to this rare bird's somber rites (for even though
  We grieved for Itys, that was long ago).   10
All birds who hover in their flight through lambent air
  But most of all, kind turtledove—despair!
For you were friends, and life was full of harmony;
  Steadfast and dedicated, you and he
Were Pylades and Agamemnon's son till death;   15
  For faithfulness, your name was shibboleth.
Yet all that trust and all that color rich and rare,
  That talking talent quick beyond compare—
What good were they? Or that you pleased her from the start?
  Glory of birds, Fate's clearly stilled your heart,   20
Despite the way your wings made emeralds look pale green.
  Your Punic-red beak wore a saffron sheen.
No bird on earth could mimic human speech like you,
  Lisping those words the way no bird could do.
Fate's envy did you in who never sought a battle;   25
  O parrot, love and peace were all your prattle.

Look how the quail choose other quail for fights and rage.
    Maybe that's why they often reach old age!
You thrived on almost nothing, loving mostly speech,
    Lacking leisure to dare to eat a peach.   30
One nut was dinner, and some poppy seeds meant sleep.
    Mere drops drove off a thirst not very deep.
The ravenous vulture lives, as do the kites that gyre.
    The daw remains alive, that rain-cloud flier,
As does the raven that Minerva hates—lives on,   35
    And barely dies, nine generations gone.
And yet that image of the human voice is dead—
    Her parrot, gifted from the Ganges' head.
The best die young, by greedy hands; they are the first
    To go, while years and years attend the worst.   40
Thersites saw Protesilaus in the earth.
    Hector, now ash, surpassed his brothers' worth.
Why mention how my fearful darling prayed for you
    With vows the South Wind blew to Timbuktu?
Then came the seventh dawn, with no more dawns behind it;   45
    You watched Fate stop her spindle, then unwind it.
And yet your weakened palate wouldn't let words die;
    Your weak tongue said, "Corinna, it's good-bye."
Beneath a hill, black ilex stands. Elysian trees—
    And earth—grow vibrant green eternities.   50
Believing doubtful things, we hear, "Good birds go there."
    (Dead dirty birds get sent some otherwhere.)
There, harmless swans feed far afield—the Bird of Fire,
    Too, who's one of a kind and can't expire.
There, Juno's peacocks fan their tails; two fowls that love—   55
    Two mating pigeons—coo; dove kisses dove.
This parrot is received there in that grove. The birds

Flock faithfully, converted by his words.
A mound his corpse's size covers the unfletched bone.
     These scanty verses match his little stone: 60
SHE LOVED ME WELL, WHICH FROM THIS TOMB CAN BE INFERRED.
MY SPEECH MADE ME MORE LEARNÈD THAN MERE BIRD.

II.7

So now you want me charged forever with fresh crimes?
     Weary, I've fought and won so many times.
If I've surveyed the marble gods, you pick some skirt
     Out of that crowd and claim that I'm a flirt.
Or if some glowing silent beauty's glanced my way,   5
     "Those tacit looks are secret signs," you say.
I praise a girl, I'm out of luck; you claw my hair.
     But if I don't, "What are you hiding there?"
My ruddy cheeks must mean—you claim—that I've grown cold,
     Though if I'm pale, I "pine for love," you scold.   10
God, how I wish I knew that I had done some wrong,
     Since guilty men can bear it if they're strong.
But you accuse without a cause, believing all—
     Till every charge made only makes them small.
Look how the poor, sad, badly-beaten donkey plods   15
     Because his masters wouldn't spare their rods!
And yet another charge? Cypassis, who has styled
     Your hair so well, has left your bed defiled?
Dear gods, were I to sin, and *she* were what you gave
     Me, where's the pleasure in some sordid slave?   20
I mean, what free man wants a slave girl's love? To hold
     A servant's whip-scarred back would leave me cold.
Besides, her only job's to dress your hair—a task

She pleases with. That's all that you could ask.
So why would I seduce your more-than-faithful maid,   25
    Only to end up spurned and then betrayed?
I swear by Venus and her wingèd little son:
    I can't confess to what I haven't done.

II.8

You ought to dress the hair of goddesses, Cypassis!
    Skilled in a thousand styles no maid surpasses,
You've made me see you're far from dull at furtive love,
    Deceiving one whom *you're* the mistress of.
But who's the snitch who pointed out this little fling,   5
    Tipping Corinna to our trafficking?
Could I have blushed? Or let some idle comment slip,
    Giving the game away with careless lip?
Suppose I *did* say men would have to be insane
    To fall for someone tethered by a chain?   10
Thessalian Achilles burned to have one; so
    Did Agamemnon (to their utter woe).
And since compared to them I'm someone almost base,
    Why should the two of us be a disgrace?
Yet when her furious eyes made you their *idée fixe*,   15
    I saw how solid blusher dyed your cheeks.
Remember, though, how brazenly I swore by Venus,
    "Corinna! No one's ever come between us"?
(Great Goddess, make the South Wind sweep all lies to sea—
    Even that one small fib that I told thee!)   20
It's time, Cypassis, and the sweet price you must pay
    Me for my services? Make love—today!
Dark ingrate, you deny me. Why? These "fears" are fakes;

To win *one* master's love is all it takes.
But if you're stubborn, then I swear I'll tell her all   25
        We did, and stand the victim for my fall.
Cypassis, watch me say how often, where, and when
        We've met and loved. We'll see what happens then!

II.9a

O Cupid, who can never be too much abused—
        Who sit here in my heart, your power unused—
Why wound just me? I've always fought your fights and flown
        Your flag, so why this hurt? My camp's your own!
Why torch your friends or shoot them with that stupid bow?   5
        Wouldn't you rather brag you beat your *foe*?
Even Achilles healed the man his spear ran through,
        So if *he* played the surgeon; why can't you?
A hunter chasing down and catching prey that flees
        Will leave it for the next prey that he sees.   10
But wholly yours, we people feel your weapons, Lord;
        Against your foes, your hand won't lift a sword!
What good's it do to blunt your barbs on bones so bare
        (Bare bones are all you've left me with, I swear)?
So many men lack love, the same love women lack;   15
        Go triumph *there*; *that's* where you should attack.
If Rome had not gone on to conquer foreign lands,
        There'd only be straw huts where marble stands.
Retired soldiers get sent out to farms they've earned,
        And thoroughbreds to pastures are returned.   20
Old worn-out, dry-docked ships of pine at last are moored;
        Old gladiators earn a wooden sword.
So why not me? I've fought Love's wars without surcease,
        But now I'm done; it's time I lived in peace.

II.9b

If some god said, "Live loveless," I would tell him no.
    Fine girls are sweet, but wicked though.
Even when I've been sick of love, all passion spent,
    Some storm comes up to torture and torment.
A rider on a bolting horse, with foaming bit,   5
    I'm rein-less in the saddle where I sit.
Picture a ship almost in port: half-touching land,
    It's blown to sea by winds it can't withstand.
That's how the random gales of Cupid batter me
    When he takes up his well-known weaponry.   10
Run me through, boy! I stand now sans my sword and spear,
    The target for your right hand. Pierce me here;
Your arrows come, and with a will they stab my breast;
    Your quiver's not a place they choose to rest.
That man's a wretch who sleeps all night and thinks he's wise   15
    Because such indolence is life's great prize.
Dumb dolt! What else is sleep but cold death's private face?
    Soon he will sleep where none do there embrace.
No, all I need to hear are words that tease and toy
    To know that even hope's a certain joy.   20
Let her wheedle, tease me, whine, or chide all day;
    I'll love her still—even when chased away.
Uncertain Mars makes wars unsure because you set
    Him bad examples that mislead him yet.
You're light as air, with wings as weightless as a bird's,   25
    Giving and taking with two-timing words.
But lovely Venus, listen; Cupid, hear: come rule
    My steadfast heart. I am your loyal fool.
And pretty women, too, should yield (though far too vain);
    Two subject sexes then will cheer your reign!   30

II.10

Graecinus, I remember you're the one who swore
    That men could love just one, and not one more.
Well, thanks to you, I'm done for and defenseless, man;
    I love two girls; who knows how it began?
The both of them are gorgeous, elegant, and chic—   5
    A pair at par, yet equally unique.
Well, maybe one is prettier, but which one is it?
    They please the same and each one is exquisite.
I veer about and come about, a windblown yacht;
    First *A*, then *B*: I love; I love her not.   10
Venus (their cause): why do my endless sorrows double?
    Wasn't one enough of woman trouble?
Why star a teeming sky, or leaf a bursting tree?
    Why rain more water on a boundless sea?
And yet . . . I need my loves; it's for my enemy   15
    To live a life of loveless chastity.
My enemies can sleep in empty beds and moan,
    Sprawling on spacious pallets all alone.
I'd settle for a savage love to wreck my slumber
    And bring me partners I can't hope to number.   20
I love those storms—as long as every girl's allowed.
    (If *one* won't do, then *two*! I'm not *that* proud!)
And I can handle love; I'm strong and lean, not weak.
    Size doesn't count; it's how you *use* physique.
Besides, the sheer delight of love just makes me stronger.   25
    No girl's alive who didn't want me longer.
(I've lasted out the longest hours of the night,
    Refreshed and ready for a bedroom fight.)
Yes, happy is the man whom Venus' strife lays low!

God, make it so; that's how *I* want to go! 30
Let soldiers bristle like a porcupine, all gory
    From arrows, if they want eternal glory.
Let lying merchants drink the sea they ploughed with greed,
    Drowning where avarice never sowed a seed.
As far as I'm concerned, I'll die in love's embrace, 35
    Melting away at a delightful pace.
Then mourners at my funeral can say of me,
    "Your death and life were matched . . . and meant to be!"

II.11

Man first learned how to sail when pine—Mt. Pelion's tree—
    Was cut and launched in the astonished sea.
Rashly, it ran for Colchis through the crashing rocks
    And got the famous fleece from golden flocks.
Too bad the *Argo* never drank the drink and sank, 5
    For if it had, we'd have the sea to thank.
Look how Corinna leaves behind her bed and gods,
    Ready to sail cruel seas against all odds!
Oh, how I'll fear what winds can do—the East and West.
    I pray the South is calm, the North at rest. 10
Out there at sea, you won't see woods or charming towns!
    Sky-blue is all you'll see—and blue sea drowns.
No shining painted shell is glittering in the deep,
    Nor pretty pebbles you might want to keep.
Girls, let your stone-white feet leave light sand prints behind; 15
    Don't go beyond. Beyond the berm, we're blind.
Let other voices tell you of the winds at war;
    Of Scylla and Charybdis' either/or;
Of rocks where threatening Ceraunia juts its chin;

Of Syrtes' sandbars, keen to do you in.   20
Believe it all, whatever others say; belief
    Means there's a chance you may not come to grief.
Too late to look back at the land when lines are cast
    Away, and seaward keels are racing fast.
Too late when leery sailors, spotting storm winds rise,   25
    See watery death in one another's eyes.
If Triton blew the waves apart with one great blast,
    Corinna, would your lovely color last?
You'd cry out for the halcyon stars, for Leda's twins:
    "The safest sea voyage never begins!"   30
Lucky are girls who cling to books and bed and land,
    Strumming Thracian lyres that they take in hand.
But if the wind should blow my fearful words away,
    May Galatea bless your sailing day.
And should you fail her, goddess Nereids, the blame   35
    Will fall on you and on your sire the same.
Remember me in going, and may that fair breeze
    Returning you blow stronger on the seas.
May mighty Nereus roll the waters home; may clear,
    Fair winds then bless the billows; bring her here.   40
Corinna, pray that Zephyr fill your canvas full,
    Then lend a hand yourself, to trim and pull.
I'll be the first on land to sight your ship and shout,
    "My love's come home! My gods have come about!"
Embraced, you'll face a hundred kisses. Who'll inflict them?   45
    The man who kills, in thanks, a votive victim.
I'll shape a sandy couch, the best that I am able;
    Whatever sand can do will do for table.
When Bacchus is decanted, oh what tales there'll be:
    Of how your bark was nearly lost at sea;   50

Of how you braved the night, your would-be enemy,
    And met the South Wind with defiant glee.
And I'll believe it all—though both of us are liars.
    Why not be flattered by our own desires?
O Lightborn shining prime, high prince of Heaven's power: 55
    Let loose your stallions' reins to haste that hour!

II.12

Come crown my head with winners' bays! My victory?
    I've triumphed, and Corinna lies with me!
So many enemies—her husband, guard, and door—
    Once kept her from my art. But now, no more;
I've earned a special triumph for this victory   5
    Won free of bloodshed, free from trickery.
It's not some little town with shallow moats I've won;
    A girl—that's what my generalship has done!
When Troy was lost—a ten-years war that killed and bled it—
    Atrides and his soldiers shared the credit.   10
My glory's mine alone and no one else's fate—
    A triumph none but I can celebrate.
I led the troops on toward this goal, a one-man force;
    I bore the flag; I was the foot and horse.
I had no luck to help me; everything I did,   15
    I did alone. Come, Triumph, as I bid!
My *casus belli*'s old: but for Tyndareus' daughter,
    There would have been no minor Asian slaughter.
Without a woman, why would Lapith and Centaur
    Have drunk the wine, then wallowed in such gore?   20
And over someone's wife the Trojans—once again—
    Went off to war, in good Latinus' reign.

Brides sent their sires to kill the Roman men they'd wed
    When Rome was young. Their cruel sword-hands ran red.
I've seen two bulls lock horns for some snow-white young cow ...   25
    Who stood and stared and stirred them to the row.
Like these, I march to Cupid's drum, but shall not kill.
    I am the humble ensign of his will.

II.13

Her womb's burden—Corinna tried to tear it out,
    And now she lies there with her life in doubt.
The anger she deserves I will not let her hear;
    It's useless now, and yields before my fear.
That she conceived must be my fault—or so I guess   5
    (I often take a *could be* for a *yes*).
Goddess of Paraetonium, of Canopus' fields,
    Of Memphis and the palms rich Pharos yields:
Isis, you love the Nile that from its bed runs free,
    Through seven delta mouths, to join the sea.   10
I beg you, by your sistrum, by Anubis' face
    (May great Osiris grant your rites his grace,
And sluggish serpents glide around your altar treasure,
    While bull-horned Apis treads the ritual measure),
Queen Isis, see us. Spare her and you spare me, too!   15
    She'll give to me the life she has from you.
So many times, Corinna's kept your feast-day rite
    Where laurels circle round your temple site.
Ilithyia, come as well. You nurse girls through
    The secret labor tearing them in two.   20
In kindness, come. Corinna needs what you can give
    Her mortal soul: the order that she live.

Do this, and dressed in white, I'll cense your altar sweet
　　With smoke and lay rich offerings at your feet.
A plaque shall read: "NASO, FOR HIS CORINNA SPARED!"　　　　25
　　Give me the cause, and all shall be prepared.
And you, my darling, if I may while life's at stake:
　　Oh, let this struggle be the last you make.

II.14

What good is it that girls need never go to war
　　Or wear a shield or march in columns or
Bow down to Mars, if they take out a bloody knife
　　And blind the womb that bears a fated life?
The first who ever tried to cut away her child　　　　5
　　Deserved to die for what she had defiled.
How could it be that *stretch marks* make for such disgust
　　That you become like killers palled in dust?
Had mankind's mothers been so selfish, mean, and base,
　　There never would have been a human race,　　　　10
And we'd have needed, one more time, some pair to throw
　　Pebbles behind them, so mankind might grow.
Who would have ruined Priam if the mother of
　　Achilles hadn't borne her child with love?
If Ilia hadn't given Romulus his birth,　　　　15
　　How could eternal Rome have ruled the earth?
Had Venus ripped Aeneas from her, such a deed
　　Would orphan us of Caesars in our need.
You, too, Corinna, born so pretty: you'd have died
　　If your mother had done what you just tried.　　　　20
And *me!* (Though I'll die from romantic love's excess).
　　My mother gave me life by saying yes.

Why strip the vine of grapes just as it starts to climb,
    Not even drinking wine before its time?
Ripe fruit drops on its own; better a life that's late   25
    Than death! So great a prize, so brief a wait!
And yet your weapons go on gouging out the wombs
    That poisons make your children's early tombs.
We hate Medea for the blood she's splattered with—
    Her babes'—and grieve for Itys in the myth.   30
Child killers that they *were*, at least they had some cause,
    Ruining their men by blood that broke all laws.
Where is *your* Tereus? Where's the Jason who demands
    You pierce your innards with a mother's hands?
Armenian tigresses won't do what women will;   35
    No lioness will see her cub and kill,
Though girls of nineteen do—but not without a price
    (Abortion doubles human sacrifice).
Then she is borne away to burn, her hair undone,
    To cries of "serves her right!" from everyone.   40
But let *my* words dissolve, and heaven blow away
    The awful burden of these things I say.
Dear gods, allow her—once—to sin and still survive;
    Two sins, and she need not be kept alive.

II.15

Go, little ring, and circle round the finger of
    My darling. All your value comes from love
That lives to please her as she puts you on right then
    And there, and thinks of joy—and me!—again.
Cling tightly to the one who fits me, snugly curled;   5
    It's only fitting you're her perfect world.

A lucky ring, to feel Corinna's coming touch!
    I envy such a band so very much.
If only I could be my own gift, courtesy
    Of Circe or of Proteus, and free   10
To let my body touch my pretty mistress' breast
    And drop down in her dress to find my nest!
I'd slip away and fall, no matter how she filled me—
    A miracle in cleavage that has thrilled me.
Likewise, to seal her letters from some prying eye   15
    (And stop my stone from stripping wax gone dry),
Thirsty, I'd kiss her liquid lips, and from them borrow
    Drops for letters that wouldn't cause me sorrow.
And if you meant me for your gem box, I would fight—
    I'd be a kind of shackle clamped down tight.   20
My Life, I'd be no shameful jewel for you to wear,
    No burden that your hand could scarcely bear.
Warm waters in the Roman baths would do no harm
    Beneath the bezel; save such false alarm
For when I rise because my eyes have seen you stripped.   25
    Though just a ring, I'd be a man equipped!
But why this wish for what I cannot have? Go, ring—
    And make her feel the passion that you bring.

II.16

I'm here in Sulmo—it's Paelignia's healthy third,
    And small, but many running streams are heard.
Sometimes the sunlight cracks the coat of summer's earth,
    And scorching Sirius shines for all it's worth.
But still the waters wander through these tender fields   5
    Where fertile things grow green in verdant yields.

The grain is good, the grapevine better. Here and there,
    Pallas's trees show olives to the air,
And in this place where sedges line the banks of streams,
    The rich soil lies; the meadow grassland teems.   10
But, oh, my darling's missing, though—something I said.
    She's far away, and my heart's blazing red.
I would not wish my days to be star-spent between
    The Twins if you were nowhere to be seen.
Let them lie deep in earth, pressed down by clay-filled loads,   15
    Those men who scarred the world with endless roads!
They might have better sent young girls to go with men,
    If all those cuts were needed way back when.
Then if I were to march some freezing Alpine trail,
    And *she* were there, no blizzard could prevail.   20
My mistress with me, I could cross the Syrtes' bar;
    South winds could rip my sails from sprit and spar.
No barking beasts in Scylla's groin, their jaws agape,
    Could scare me, nor Malea's jutting cape.
I wouldn't fear Charybdis, drunk on sunken ships   25
    And spewing spouts to catch in loathsome lips!
But if the winds of Neptune rise and overturn
    The helping sea-gods carved out on the stern,
Just put your soft white arms around my shoulders and
    I'll bear your body's burden safe to land.   30
Leander swam, lamp-led, to reach his Hero's side,
    And once more would have . . . had the light not died.
But lacking you—though I have vineyards all around;
    Though rippling brooks are lacing Sulmo's ground,
And peasants bring the waters irrigating crops,   35
    And cool tree-breezes kiss their leafy tops—
I feel I'm not on wholesome old Paelignian earth,

Nor in my father's land that saw my birth,
But Scythia, Cilicia, Britannia; with
   Rock-chained Prometheus in his bloody myth.   40
Well, elms love vines and vines are bound to climbing elms,
   So why are we exiled to separate realms?
You swore to be my marching mate forever, dear,
   By me and by your eyes—my stars down here.
But leaves outweigh a woman's words; for all they're worth,   45
   A wind—a wave—would wipe them off the earth.
Yet pity poor, abandoned me, if you still can,
   And suit your deeds to words to save this man.
Take up your ponies' reins as soon as you are able,
   Then whip them as they're flying out the stable.   50
And may the hills lie down for her—flat, smooth, and fast,
   As easy valleys watch her racing past.

II.17

If anyone believes a slave to women base,
   I'm gladly guilty of that sweet disgrace!
But I don't *care*, so long as she consumes me mildly—
   Great Venus, queen whose isles waves batter wildly.
If only I'd been captured by some kindly dear;   5
   But this one's only beautiful, I fear.
Beauty makes her haughty . . . so I'm in her spell.
   Poor me! She knows her beauty far too well,
Deriving her hauteur from what her mirror shows.
   (She won't look till her painted visage glows.)   10
But even if your charms mean pride (and promise capture),
   Despite such charms that send me into rapture,
Don't scorn my looks because I can't compare with you.

Worse things with better *can* go two by two.
The poet says Calypso, ravished by a man,   15
     Kept him against his will to delve (she span);
That Peleus wed the sea-born child of Nereus,
     And law-wise Numa wed Egeria.
Vulcan's been matched with Venus, but that's pretty rich
     (His step's a short-legged limp). Now *there's* a hitch!   20
This very verse is mismatched, but the six-foot line
     Marries the five-foot one and does just fine.
You, too, my light. Take me on any terms you set;
     Command me like some Forum advocate.
You won't regret it, and you'll cry when I go out—   25
     We'll make a love beyond all fear and doubt.
These songs composed with elegance are all my treasures,
     And lots of girls crave fame . . . sung to my measures.
One says that *she's* Corinna (but she's not—I know).
     What would she not have paid to have it so?   30
But cold Eurotas and the far-off, poplared Po
     Flow separately, and twin banks keep them so.
You'll be the only one, my sole and guiding light—
     The single Muse inspiring all I write.

II.18

Macer, while you've been versing toward Achilles' rage
     And arming warlords for that war's first stage,
Naso's been lolling in Queen Venus' lazy shade,
     And Love has stopped each serious stab I've made.
I've told my girl to leave at least a thousand times,   5
     But when I have, into my lap she climbs!
I've said so often, "I'm ashamed"; she fights back tears,
     Replying, "Shame? I can't believe my ears!"

Of course, she promptly throws her arms around my neck
    With scads of kisses, till my heart's a wreck.   10
I'm lost, and summon genius from assumptions of
    These arms to write of battles born of love.
But still I snatched at sceptres, crafting tragedy,
    Which went quite well (I'm good at it, you see).
Love laughed, though, at the actor's cloak and painted boots   15
    And royal wand my hand so poorly suits.
My mistress won me, though (for her, not very hard);
    Soon, Cupid conquered him a buskined bard.
I do my best, singing the arts that I've professed,
    But find myself a man who's self-oppressed.   20
Sometimes, I write the words Penelope once sent,
    Or sobbing Phyllis's abandonment.
I write to Paris, Jason, and Macareus;
    To Theseus and his son Hippolytus.
I write the words that Dido writes with blade in hand.   25
    And I've been Sappho, by Phaon unmanned.
How soon Sabinus wrote replies from all these men!
    At earth's four corners, he took up his pen.
(Penelope the Shining knows Ulysses' seal,
    And Phaedra reads what Phaedra ought to feel.   30
Aeneas writes to his dismissed Elissa; here—
    If Phyllis lives—Demophoon's words appear
(And even wretched Jason's to Hypsipyle);
    Requited, Sappho sends her lyre to thee,
Phoebus. Macer, you've versed of love as I have—one   35
    Minute it's Mars; the next, it's Venus' son.
There's Helen and her man—two cheaters too well known,
    With true Laodamia, dead and gone.
If I know you, you'd sooner *not* the epic line,
    But Love's. Come. Cross from your camp into mine.   40

II.19

Guard her for me, if not for you; bolt her door,
    You dolt. That way, I'll want her all the more.
(*Easy* doesn't do it; hurdles are what we need!
    He's iron if he loves what men *concede*.)
Let lovers hope and fear; a spurning every now   5
    And then will give a man a cause to vow.
What do I care for Chance that never plays a trick?
    I can't love what won't cut me to the quick!
Cunning Corinna saw this weakest link in me,
    And worked it for my heart's captivity.   10
How many times she's had "a headache"—nothing wrong—
    And ordered tardy me to "get along"!
So often has she given accusations vent
    And played the scold when I was innocent!
Then, firing up my torch again, she'd be my friend,   15
    Smiling on vows protested without end.
How sweet and winning were her words and ways and kisses
    (Great god—more than any Miss or Mrs.!).
Now you, my newfound dear who've won my wandering eye,
    Pretend some fear . . . and when I beg, deny.   20
Please let me stretch out on your threshold. Let me feel
    The cold nights; bind me on their frosty wheel.
That way, my love grows hardy through the times to come,
    Nourished by that which it's been severed from.
For love grown fat will cloy us with its tedium,   25
    The way sweet cake can kill us, crumb-by-crumb.
If Danae had never walked her brazen tower,
    Would Jove have brought her to her birthing hour?
And Juno, guarding hornèd Io, clearly erred;

Jove thought that made her sweetest of the herd!   30
Who wants an easy love can pick leaves off a tree,
    Or drink from running streams abundantly.
But girls who mean to rule for long should learn to cheat . . .
    Though spare *me*, clement gods, from such deceit.
Whatever happens, then, the easy's not for me: 35
    What flees, I follow; what follows, I flee.
So careless husband, listen! Lock her up; begin
    Closing your door when dusk comes drifting in.
Start asking who it is comes knocking, rapping, tapping,
    And why the still night fills with watchdogs' yapping.   40
Start looking at those notes her servant shuffles back
    And forth—and what it is your bed sheets lack.
It's time for canker-cares to gnaw away *your* marrow,
    Yielding a field for *me* to plough and harrow.
Only the thief who steals sand from an empty beach   45
    Can love a girl her husband keeps in reach.
I'm warning you! If you don't lock her in a vault,
    My interest in her crashes to a halt!
I've put up with this state of things too long, I hope,
    And mean to cuckold me some *vigilant* dope.   50
You're so damned slow, and oh, the things you're guilty of!
    This dumb complaisance means that I can't love.
I'm sad to see you never mean to lock me out.
    Will nighttime always kill my fear and doubt,
No vengeance as the evening comes to make me sigh,   55
    Compelling me to pray that you would die?
Who wants a rival who is such an easy mark,
    Just giving in . . . and putting out love's spark?
Oh, why not find some other dolt to be your foe,
    You want *me* for a rival, just say no.   60

BOOK III

III.1

Unlogged for untold years, there is a grove of pine
    Not hard to think the haunt of the divine.
A sacred spring comes up beside a cave, rock-hung;
    Early and late, sweet birds have always sung.
Below that forest roof, while walking fro and to,   5
    I wondered what my Muse would have me do.
Then Elegy arrived, perfumed and coifed for sport;
    One foot was long though, and the other short.
Her face beamed love; her form was fine; thin was her dress.
    Yet one foot-fault made extra loveliness!   10
Then Tragedy comes stalking in. Her dark locks fall
    Across her brow; the ground's swept by her pall.
Her left hand wielded what was Drama's regal wand,
    Which matched the Lydian buskins she had donned.
This queen spoke first: "You'll always love, so it would seem,   15
    And play the poet of that endless theme?
By now, your sins, which each low soak and sponger's glossed,
    Ring out where every Roman road is crossed.
Rome's plain folk point The Poet out; you've been indexed
    As He Whom Love Has Singed—and Oversexed.   20
So unaware, you're Topic Number One in Rome,
    Bragging of all you've done in every poem.
It's time to try some nobler, higher theme beyond

What Bacchus has inspired with his wand.
Your matter matters too much; use your skill! Sing out   25
    About great deeds. Say, 'This makes my soul shout!'
Right now, you use your Muse to string young girls along;
    Your youth's first youthful measures are all wrong.
Now lend *me*, Roman Tragedy, a famous name,
    Filling my needs with your bright spirit's flame."   30
So, regal in her painted boots, that much she said,
    Three or four times shaking her thick-curled head.
The other one, I think, then grinned a sidelong glance
    (Was that a myrtle wand by any chance?)
"Proud Tragedy, you tax us with a wordy levy,   35
    Oppressing those who find you proud and heavy.
And yet yourself you've used these elegiac feet,
    Attacking with a six- and five-foot beat.
I won't attempt to rank your lofty lines with mine;
    Rich doors beside poor doors are far too fine.   40
I'm lightweight, and my charge, Eros, is lightweight, too.
    Singing my theme, I never overdo.
Yet Cupid's mother, lacking me, is just some jade;
    To be her pander—that's why I was made.
The door you can't kick in despite that tragic boot   45
    Collapses when I plead my sweetest suit.
And yet I earned this greater power. I let my brow
    Bear loads your haughty brow would not allow.
I've taught Corinna how to catch her guard off-guard
    And breach a faithful door. It wasn't hard.   50
She now knows how to shuck her slip and slip away,
    Padding the tiles—a girl no steps betray.
So many times have I been hung, pinned down to doors,
    Nakedly read by bustling mobs of boors!

One time, I waited in sheer agonies of fear   55
    Inside a slave's cloak till the coast was clear.
Oh, I remember how, a birthday present, I
    Was rent by her, my torn scraps flushed bye-bye.
But I was first to stir your stylus, plant the seed;
    You've *me* to thank *she* pays you any heed."   60
When she was done, I said, "I pray you, both and each,
    Open the ears my timid words would reach.
One honors me with sceptre and with buskin; stirred,
    My tongue is touched, and waits with mighty word.
The other names our winning love The Sport of It;   65
    Well, add long verses to the short of it!
And Tragedy, give me some space a little while.
    You take so long; love fits a briefer style."
Convinced, she heard my prayer. Coy mistresses, come here;
    I'm free, but fear Time's wingèd drawing near.   70

III.2

"I'm not here for the horses, dear, but that's no sin
    (I'd even celebrate, should your team win).
I came so I could talk with you and sit with you
    And make you see I love you (yes, I do!).
You watch the horses; I watch you. Each gets to gaze   5
    At what he loves; four hungry eyes may graze.
The driver that you favor, he's a lucky man.
    So *that's* the one that no man's luckier than?
I wish that were *my* fate. I'd let them burst the gate,
    That team, then lash them to a hellish rate,   10
Whipping their backs and withers, giving them their head,
    The turnpost splinters shaving their flanks red.

But spotting you in mid-career, I know I'd stop.
    I'd lose the loosened reins; they'd slip and drop.
(As loving Pelops, often almost stricken by a   15
    Pisaean spear, adored Hippodamia.
Yet Pelops won because she backed him on that course.
    May all our lovers pick the proper horse!)
Why pull away, my dear? This seating crowds us tight;
    The Circus may be tight, but that's all right!   20
Hey! Whosis on the right there: watch those elbows, churl.
    Those are *her* ribs you're poking; that's *my* girl!
And you behind: scrunch up those legs. Discretion, please.
    Just keep them to yourself, those bony knees.
But look, my dear: your cloak is dragging in the dust—   25
    A thing my hands could easily adjust.
A jealous cloak, to keep such lovely legs all wrapped!
    The more one looks, the more that someone's trapped.
They're legs like Atalanta's. Fleeing with those charms,
    She kept herself from Melanion's arms.   30
They are Diana's thighs in paintings, skirts hiked high
    As she pursued her prey while giving cry.
I've longed to see your legs; I have! You're fire
    To flame; you're water, and the sea grows higher!.
Surely that proves that other sights may satisfy,   35
    Whatever charms beneath your thin gown lie.
Till then, I sense that you would like a gentle fan?
    Then put one in my hand, and I'm your man.
Or is this heat far more *my* heat, and not the air?
    Is lady-love the flame that's burning there?   40
But while I'm babbling, your white dress has caught some dust.
    Leave her, dust. Depart that snow-white bust.
Now comes procession-pomp; be still, pay heed, and clap.

Then next, that gold parade without a gap.
First, Nike, carried high, wings spread, in pride of place.   45
    Goddess, draw near; may my love win this race!
Applaud for Neptune, all you sea-besotted band.
    No seas for me; I'm partial to the land.
Soldiers, applaud for Mars; give love of war release.
    Peace pleases me . . . and love that lives in peace.   50
The hunter's Phoebe's next, then Phoebus, who's for seers.
    Now craftsmen cheer Minerva who appears.
Cheer Ceres and cheer Bacchus, hicks who plough with bullocks.
    Horsemen, cry out for Castor; boxers, Pollux.
Venus, we clap for you and Cupid with his bow   55
    Look on my work . . . and let your favor show.
Oh, steer my new dear right; may she have loving—mine!"
    A nod was all I needed for a sign.
"Now darling, give me what that lovely goddess gave:
    The leave to speak. Then I shall be your slave.   60
By all these witnesses, and by the gods, I mean
    To have you for all time, to be my queen!
But dear, your legs are dangling! Why not tuck your feet
    Into the grate? Now *that's* a comfy seat!
The circus grounds are cleared now for the featured show.   65
    The praetor's sprung the teams, and off they go
From staggered starting stalls! The man you back of course is
    The one who'll win; all know—even the horses.
Oh, no! He's driven round the turnpost way too wide!
    You dolt! That axle-grazer's pulled inside   70
And leads now, cretin! Do you want to break her heart?
    Yank left—hard left! Now show a driver's art!
We're cheering on a moron! Quirites: re-call!
    Demand a re-start. Throw your togas, one and all!

There! Now they're back. But lest a waving toga muss   75
　　　Your hair, hide in my cloak; come in with us.
And now they're at the post, and now they're off again.
　　　The teams race out; the drivers give them rein.
So overtake them, will you, flat out in the stretch,
　　　To please my girl—and me, you stupid wretch!   80
She wins! They heard her prayers! But mine? I must stay calm
　　　(He's won his palm. My palm still seeks her palm.)."
She smiled, then promised with her eyes (eyes say it best).
　　　I said, "Enough, dear; elsewhere, yield the rest."

III.3

I dare you: go believe in gods. She lied who swore,
　　　And yet her face is fairer than before!
Her hair, post-perjury, is every bit as long
　　　As long before she did those gods that wrong.
Before, her face shone white, suffused with beauty's glow;   5
　　　Now pink still tints those cheeks as white as snow.
Her foot was small—and still her foot is dainty-small.
　　　Once both tall and fine, she still is fine and tall.
Then, diamond-eyed; now, blessed with brilliant stars for eyes:
　　　One and the same. By these she told her lies.   10
So clearly, the eternal gods let *some* foreswear—
　　　They have their privileges, the false and fair!
I think back how she swore by her own eyes—her vow—
　　　By mine as well; it's mine that suffer now.
So tell me, gods, you gods she tricked but got off free: 15
　　　Why has *her* punishment devolved on me?
I am Andromeda, and we are both your shame,
　　　Condemned by you to bear another's blame.

Isn't it bad enough I have your worthless word?
     She's mocking us, no penalty incurred.   20
Am I to feel her pain and thus be her redeemer,
     A slaughtered lamb who saves that little schemer?
Well, either God's a weightless name the witless fear,
     Stirring up dolts who claim to see and hear,
Or else if any god exists, he's far too fond   25
     Of ingenues whose will becomes his bond.
Mars slings his sword on when he means to kill us men,
     And Pallas with her spear begins again.
Apollo's bows are bent on us; Jove's high right hand
     Is aimed at us, lightning at his command.   30
But even injured gods don't dare offend the fair,
     Frightened of girls who give them not a care.
Who'd want to burn sweet coals to gods of ashen pallor?
     Surely *men* should show some manly valor!
Yet Jupiter will burn his bolts through forts and groves,   35
     But never singe the lying girls he loves.
So many have deserved what Semele once got
     (A fate she earned; to burn—that was her lot).
For if she'd only sent that red-hot love away,
     Bacchus might have been born some other way.   40
Oh, why before the gods these whining, plaintive arts—
     And threats? Gods, too have eyes—gods, too, have hearts.
If I were God myself, I'd let all girls go free
     Whose forsworn tongues defamed divinity.
I'd swear all girls spoke truth, so none would think it odd   45
     To see I was no strictly rigid god.
But darling, don't abuse the gifts of deities:
     Spare me my eyes, at least, I beg you please.

III.4

Husband: to watch and ward your wife? That's far too hard—
  And doesn't work. Her heart should be her guard.
If, kept from fear, she's chaste, then chastely she begins;
  Who doesn't sin because she can't, still sins!
For if you guard the body well, the will's there still,   5
  And no one "saves" a girl against her will—
Not even if you turn the key in every lock.
  Sin stays within no matter whom you block.
For those *unchecked* stray less; free chance to sin
  Means cheating's far less likely to begin.   10
Trust me! Stop spurring on affairs by what's forbid;
  You'll keep her home by giving her her head.
Just yesterday I saw a horse who fought his bit
  Outrunning lightning in a foaming fit.
But then he halted at the slackening of the rein;   15
  The lines let loose lay on his streaming mane.
That's how it is; we want what we're denied. We think
  Like feverish men who crave what's bad to drink.
Yes, Argus had a hundred eyes, both front and rear;
  But Cupid proved he wasn't such a seer.   20
Her iron-guarded bedroom, strongest on the earth,
  Could not keep Danae from giving birth.
Penelope, unguarded, still stayed undefiled,
  Despite so many suitors young and wild.
"Forbidden" is a Siren; locked gates beg for thieves,   25
  And easy booty's what a burglar leaves.
It's not your lady's charms that make your rivals care;
  They see *you* love her. Something must be there!
Guarding your girl won't make her chaste—just more desired;

Not charms, but lovers' fear—that's what's required.   30
Be angry if you like, but *outlawed* joys persuade;
    She only charms if she says, "I'm afraid!"
(Of course, you can't *imprison* the nobility;
    Let low-born women suffer lock and key.)
Why keep her chaste just so her guard can say, "*I did it*,"   35
    As if such "faithfulness" were to *his* credit?
Adultery's a thing that only shocks the hicks,
    Who know too little of our city tricks
(There's Romulus, who's Ilia's boy, and Ilia's Remus—
    Mars' bastards both and equally as famous).   40
If chastity was such a must, why is your wife
    So beautiful? They never mix in life.
So let your lady have her fancy; don't look stern
    Or act the rigid husband. Live and learn!
But court the friends your wife brings home—she'll fetch a lot.   45
    So little effort, but look what you've got!
You'll party with the finest boys that ever were—
    Enjoying gifts you never gave to her!

III.5

"Then once upon a night, my eyes sank down in sleep,
    And what I saw was terror, dark and deep.
Below a sun-drenched hill, a grove of holly stood,
    Abundant birds half hiding in that wood.
Hard by, a grassy meadow, green as any green,   5
    And fresh from gently talking streams unseen.
Below the boughs, I sought out shade from heat I fought,
    But heat stayed there, below the shade I sought.
Then lo! A snow-white heifer, coming there to feed

On flowered grass stood plainly in that mead—   10
Whiter than shining snow that only now came down,
    And time had not yet turned to verb from noun.
Her gleaming was like milk, still foaming in the pail
    And fresh from ewes drained dry that quake and quail.
Companioned by a bull, she'd found her happy mate,   15
    A pair that lent the tender ground their weight.
Now while he lay at ease, re-ruminating food
    And chewing his cud in a thoughtful mood,
It seemed I saw sleep cradle down his nodding head
    Till heavy horns and all had found their bed.   20
Then down a crow came, planing lightly through the air,
    And landed on that green, chattering there.
He struck with thorny beak against the heifer's breast,
    Then flew a few white tufts back to his nest.
And though she lingered by her bull, he lay marooned   25
    At last; she wandered off, a livid wound
Upon her breast. She'd seen horns lowered to the ground
    Some ways away, where fodder could be found,
(Yes, other bulls). The white cow ran to join that herd
    And crop the greener grass her heart preferred.   30
Now, augur, come. Come tell us, master of the night:
    What might my vision mean—and tell me right."
That's what I said. The Vision Seer of the Dark
    Then spoke, weighing with care my least remark:
"That heat you shunned beneath the shaking leaves above—   35
    But badly shunned—that was the heat of love.
The white cow was your girl—a shade that was just right—
    And you the bull, her mate, a man of might.
The crow who beaked her breast was a pandering crone
    Who turned your mistress from you for her own.   40

As for that long delay that left the bull for dead,
    It means you'll be deserted in your bed.
Those deep, dark bruises that her white hair will not hide?
    Adulterous stains that cannot be denied."
The seer was done. I froze as if my face were drained   45
    Of blood, and only deepest Night remained.

III.6

Listen, river all mucky-banked and choked with reeds:
    Slow down! I rush to meet my mistress' needs.
Unbridged, you boast no cockle boat to float my hope,
    Or unrowed ferry hauled on by a rope.
I never feared to cross those waves (if I recall)   5
    That only reached my heels—when you were small.
Now *you're* the one who's rushing, melted mountain snows,
    Rolling your roaring current as it goes.
But tell me my reward for racing here—the way
    I've barely slept; for yoking night to day—   10
If still I have to stand, that farther shore denied,
    And nothing gets me to your other side.
Right now, I want the wings that Perseus had, who slew
    Medusa, lopped her snaky locks, then flew.
Right now, I wish I had the chariot from which   15
    Demeter sowed the land, and made it rich.
But these are hoary lies that stay myths still;
    That never saw true light—and never will.
Instead, you are a river bursting from its banks.
    Long stay your course in bounds, and I'll give thanks.   20
Trust me, torrent: you'll earn a hatred bitter-black
    If people learn you held this lover back.

Rivers owe lovers much; to help should be the aim.
    Young lovers and their rivers feel the same.
Inachus paled for Melie, for Bithynia's daughter,   25
    And blanching, set a torch to icy water.
Xanthus, the siege of Troy was not yet ten years old:
    Neaera flashed her eyes . . . and stopped you cold.
And Alpheus ran Arethusa down, propelled
    By love of what Arcadian caverns held.   30
Peneus, you, too, who in Phthiotia tried to hide
    Away Creusa, Xuthus' promised bride.
Why bother mentioning Asopus, Thebe's flame—
    That child of Mars who gave five girls her name?
And Achelous: if you're asked what happened to   35
    Your horns, it's "Hercules broke one in two."
(What Calydon—and all Aetolia—could not do,
    Lone Deianira could, and won him, too.)
Even great Egypt's Nile, each outlet one wide mouth,
    That river's source deep hidden somewhere south,   40
Could not, they say, put out the fire Euanthe set;
    Asopus' daughters kept him blazing wet.
Enipeus tried to dry for Tyro, so he bid
    His stream recede, to show his bed. It did!
And Anio, too, who runs through limestone, takes the rains,   45
    And irrigates old Tibur's fruited plains.
Ilia pleased you by her ill-groomed tresses matched
    To ravaged cheeks that savage nails had scratched.
Bewailing both her uncle's crime and Mars' embraces,
    She wandered barefoot through earth's barren places.   50
But Anio saw her from his bed and made his choice,
    Rearing, and raising up his raucous voice.
Here's what he said: "Ilia, so fearful, sad, and anxious,

Idaean Ilia, why tramp on my banks thus?
What's happened to your hair? Why wander all around?   55
    Let fillets bind your hair; let it be crowned!
Why stain your eyes with tears? There is no need, my child,
    To beat your bosom with a fist gone wild.
Oh, who could watch your tears well up and yet remain
    Unmoved, his flint-like heart immune to pain?   60
Lay down your fear. My royal course I'll open here,
    With waters that adore; lay down your fear!
I'll make you queen of all my nymphs—at least five-score;
    Come rule our waters' hundred nymphs or more.
O maiden, these are gifts I pray you will not spurn,   65
    And others—richer—that you needn't earn."
That's what he said. But still with lowered look she eyed
    The ground, showering her bosom as she cried.
Three times she tried to run. Three times she stopped beside
    The waters and herself: weak; terrified.   70
But in the end, her fingers clawing cruelly at her hair,
    She trembled, telling of her heart's despair:
"I wish my virgin bones had filled our sepulchre
    When virginal was what those bones still were!
I *was* a Vestal. Why accept Lord Hymen's flame,   75
    Denied the Trojan altar fires in my shame?
Why wait for crowds to brand me with a harlot's name?
    Oh, may I die, embracing scarlet blame."
That's all that she could stand. Cloaking her tear-stained face,
    She leapt into the river's roaring race.   80
They say that fluent stream embraced her, caught her life,
    And bore her to his bed, his wedded wife.
So, river, haven't you fallen in love as well,
    But groves and coverts meant we couldn't tell?

Now even as we speak, you widen by the minute;   85
    Your bed, though deep, can't keep your currents in it.
Well, what are you to *me*? Why balk my lover's fun,
    You rustic creek? Why halt what I've begun?
Besides, who says that you're some famous river worth
    A name that spreads your fame across the earth?   90
You're only random rivulets: no name, no source,
    And nothing like a well-known watercourse.
With no fixed path, your only cause is rains and snows
    That melt—and only winter gives you those.
But even so, it's winter boom or summer bust: 95
    First torrents, then ... there's nothing there but dust.
What grateful traveler ever drank you *then*,
    Or blessed you with "Flow on till God knows when"?
Your harm the flocks and even more, the fields: such woes
    Are others', and I'm not concerned with those.   100
Oh, tell me why I told you of the mighty Nile.
    I must have been half-crazy all the while
Inachus, Achelous, and their loves went by.
    Just look at you! Shame makes me want to die.
What you deserve is what I wish you, mucky one: 105
    A world of winters filled with fierce, hot sun.

III.7

Wasn't she beautiful, a graceful girl, well-kempt?
    A girl about whom I had always dreamt?
So when I held her, why did nothing raise its head?
    I lay, a shameful load that mocked the bed.
Oh, we were lickerish all right, both equally,   5
    But she and I, somehow, could not agree.

Around my neck she threw her ivory arms as bright
    As the Sithonian snow, and twice as white.
She tongued my lazy mouth with eager kisses—sigh!—
    Then slid her lusty thigh beneath my thigh,   10
And with endearments, whispered "Master"—every term
    That worldly women use to make men firm.
But still it failed what I'd proposed, that flaccid hunk
    That froze as if from hemlock that I'd drunk.
A trunk inert: what a picture I must have made   15
    Who wasn't really human or a shade.
If I'm to know old age, what old age will I treasure,
    When right now, youth can't stand up to its measure?
I'm just ashamed that in my youth I'm young and male;
    She saw virility and youth both fail!   20
A Vestal left that bed; I hadn't touched or kissed her .
    We could have been a brother and his sister.
Mere days ago, my powers worked for Chlide—twice.
    Three times Pitho and Libas found it nice!
Corinna once demanded—and I satisfied   25
    Her—nine full measures—all nine times I tried.
Had some Thessalian potion laid my body low?
    Had herbs and charms and simples made me so?
Had some witch cursed my name with voodoo dolls of wax
    And stuck my liver's heart with prick attacks?   30
Wounded by spells, grain shrivels on the sterile stalk,
    And wells will fail when witchy women talk.
Hexed acorns rain from oaks; from spell-cast vines, grapes fall.
    Fruit drops without having been touched at all.
So maybe it was magic verses made me nervous—   35
    Or worse—and took my member out of service.
Or shame came in, perhaps—shame at what had been mine—

And added to the words that shrank my vine.
I covered her, and what a lovely girl she was.
    I mean, I touched her as her tunic does!   40
And from *her* touch, old Nestor could go on and on;
    Tithonus freshen up like brand new Dawn.
I had a girl like that, but she had no such man.
    My prayers can't help me now. Oh, what prayers can?
I think the mighty gods wish that they had refused   45
    To give me such a gift so badly used.
Clearly, I hoped she'd be receptive to my kiss.
    She was. And bedding me was not amiss.
What came of it? Not much. I was a paper king—
    A wealthy skinflint lacking just one thing.   50
I'm tell-tale Tantalus, parched in the waters' waste,
    Condemned to claw at fruit he'll never taste.
Who leaves a young girl's bed at dawn so pure that rushing
    To sacred altars doesn't leave him blushing?
But maybe she was derelict and ugly, too,   55
    Failing to kiss with every trick she knew?
Oh, no! She could have made the dumbest oak her own,
    Charmed adamant, and stirred the deafest stone.
In fact, she could have moved the least of living men.
    But I was not the living man I'd been.   60
In singing to the deaf, what good would Phemius do?
    The paintings blind Thamyras sees are few.
And yet what pleasures I had formed in my supposes
    Of tangled limbs beneath the sheets. He froze as
If he were a blighted bloom, and still he lay   65
    As if the limpest rose of yesterday.
And *now* just look! Impetuous and in position,
    He clamors for a battlefield commission!

Oh, lie down now, the worst of all our body parts!
    I've fallen too often for these fits and starts.   70
Because you trick your lord, I'm caught—an unarmed master
    Made shamefaced and depressed by this disaster.
And she agreed, my girl, who hadn't been too proud
    To take in hand a slave who only bowed.
But when she realized no art would raise this flag   75
    That lay as indolent as any rag,
She turned on me and railed: "Make fun of *me*? Who said
    You had to drop your self here on my bed?
Either some Circe's pierced a magic doll of you
    Or I'm this evening's *second* choice to woo."   80
Then up she leapt, half-wrapped in open negligee,
    A barefoot lovely as she tripped away.
And lest her maids should figure out this aftermath,
    She gave my crime scene just a little bath.

III.8

Does anyone respect the liberal arts these days,
    Or think that courting brides with verses pays?
There was a time when genius counted more than gold;
    Poor poets now are left out in the cold.
Now that my little books have pleased my mistress so,   5
    It seems *I'm* not allowed where *they* can go!
She's praised me, true, but still, I show up and get stiffed,
    To walk around in shame despite my gift.
Just look, though: nouveau riche, a knight made knight because
    Of bloodshed gets her nod; it gives you pause.   10
My Life, could you embrace a man like that, stained red
    Up to his elbows, taking *him* to bed?

In case you didn't know, a helmet hid that brow;
    A sword hung on that hip you hang on now.
That hand that wears its new gold ring so badly bore   15
    A buckler once. Yes, touch it; *smell* the gore!
And tell me: can you touch the hand that tore apart
    A life? Where is your erstwhile tender heart?
Scan all those scars, the vestiges of old campaigns:
    His body got him all his ill-got gains.   20
Maybe he'll say how many jugulars he's slashed!
    Go on! Just touch his hand. Don't be abashed!
Meanwhile, the purest priest of Phoebus and the Muses,
    I sing the useless verse your door abuses?
If so, that means the smart ones learn not what I know,   25
    But where the sharpest spears stand—and they go.
Had Homer traded epics for *these* epic wars,
    Then Homer, all love's pleasures would be yours.
Or think of Jove, who knew so well the worth of gold;
    Become a shower, he bought a girl to hold.   30
(No money meant she and her sire played hard to get
    Behind those brazen doors. She'd be there yet
If clever Jupiter had not come down like gold.
    She opened up—and did what she was told.)
But back when Saturn reigned, earth's lucre was secure   35
    Down dark and deep. Its priceless seams stayed pure,
And copper, silver, gold, and iron hid their ore,
    No precious metals then. But now, no more!
Back then, no need for ploughs, since Saturn gave his folk
    Free fruit, and honey from the hollowed oak.   40
No farmer ripped the earth with hoe and hungry share.
    Surveyors were unknown; men didn't care!
And not a single oar blade cut the virgin sea;

The littoral was mankind's boundary.
    Man*kind*? You've damned yourself by doing all you could;   45
        Your greedy genius does you no damned good.
What's been the *point* of battlements about your towns,
        As angry onagers threw stones at crowns?
What was the sea to you, or you to sky that you
        Should rule them both? One kingdom wouldn't do?   50
Now where you can, you try the skies: the temples of
        Quirinus, Bacchus, Caesar, high above.
We mine as ours the earth's false harvest—buried gold—
        While bloody army money's talk takes hold.
No Senate for the poor, but higher brackets? Yes,   55
        And knights and judges, too. God, what a mess!
Well, *let* them have it. Let Campus and Forum wait
        On those who lust for legions and the state.
Only we'd like to keep our lovers—please?—unbought.
        That wouldn't be too much ... one would have thought.   60
But now, he orders her around, my love who fends
        Me off, by virtue of the loot he spends.
And me? She listens to her client and her guard.
        One small bribe and they wouldn't be so hard!
Oh, would there were a lovers' god, though it seems not.   65
        He'd pulverize these prizes so ill-got!

III.9

If Memnon's—and Achilles'—mother ever cried;
        If goddesses have mourned great souls that died;
Then Elegy, undo your hair and sob with rue.
        From this day forth, your name will be too true.
Tibullus made your fame; he was your loyal bard   5

Who weights the bier with bones all cracked and charred.
You see how Cupid comes, his quiver upside down,
    Bow broken, and his brand left back in town?
His droopy wings announce the cloud he sorrows under;
    His small fist beats his heart (it sounds like thunder).   10
The ringlets round his neck all catch his falling tears
    Timed to concussive sobs that rack our ears.
Ascanius, at your father's wake he wept that way,
    Staggering from your house into the day.
Tibullus, Venus mourned for you no less or more   15
    Than for Adonis, gored by that wild boar.
Yes, poets are the men gods cannot live without;
    Some say those gods do hedge us all about.
Of course there's nothing holy death will not profane,
    Laying its hands on all with black disdain.   20
Ismarian Orpheus? What good did his parents do,
    Or beasts he stunned with song—if that were true?
And Phoebus sang, "O Linus, woe!" So people say.
    Deep in the woods, his lyre refused to play.
Maeonian Homer, who is like an endless spring   25
    Of things Pierian to those who sing,
Has long been dead; in black Avernus he lies drowned.
    It's only *verse* no pyre can confound.
These things endure: the poet's work; the Trojan War;
    The undone shroud Penelope'd restore.   30
So Nemesis and Delia: their names will ring.
    One was his love, one quite a recent thing.
Each sistrum struck for Isis; every altar vow;
    Your single beds! What good are all those now?
When good men die though young, I start to think—forgive   35
    My doubt!—there are no gods. For if you live

In piety, you die. Pray right, and as you pray,
    From fane to tomb, death drags you there to stay.
Believe in verse alone! Look where Tibullus lies:
    His ashes fill an urn of paltry size.   40
Dear friend, they have you now, those flames that leap and start
    And aren't afraid to feed upon your heart?
Flames capable of such an awful sin might well
    Have burnt the temples where the gods must dwell.
Venus, the queen of Eryx, had to turn away,   45
    Yielding a tear, as I have heard some say.
Yet this is better than Phaeacian earth—a plot
    You'd know alone, while all the world would not.
At least this way your mother closed your swimming eyes
    And gave your billowed ash life's final prize.   50
This way, your sister came, her hair undone and torn,
    To grieve . . . and help your shattered mother mourn.
Your pyre brought Delia, Nemesis, and others,
    To keen and kiss with cousins, sisters, brothers.
Departing, Delia said, "I knew your love, none higher;   55
    You lived as long as I remained your fire."
But Nemesis: "His loss is mine, not yours to clasp;
    His dead hand dropped when I was in his grasp."
Should more than name outlive us till some kingdom come,
    Tibullus then will see Elysium.   60
Catullus, come with Calvus. Meet that soul, and wear,
    O learned poet, ivy round your hair.
Come, Gallus, since your blood and soul you loved to spend—
    Assuming that you never sold your friend.
Your ghost is their companion; if there are such ghosts,   65
    Tibullus, you'll have added to their hosts.
Urn, guard these bones and let them sleep through endless night.
    And on his ashes, may the earth be light.

III.10

Grain's holy rites are here, and someone sleeps alone:
  So Ceres now has come, but my girl's gone.
Gold goddess, tender tresses spiked with wheaten ears,
  Your worship stops *our* rites, and interferes!
True, everywhere, "The goddess gives," the people tell us;   5
  You bless our blessings and you're never jealous.
In ancient times, who knew what parching grain was worth?
  The threshing floor was not known on this earth.
Instead, the oak, first oracle, let acorns fall.
  Men ate wild herbs with these, and that was all.   10
Then, Ceres was the first to show seeds how to bear;
  She sickled first, and cut grain's golden hair.
She was the one who bade the bull bend neck to yoke.
  Hers was the share by which the earth first broke.
So who could think that Ceres loves lone lovers' tears,   15
  Or revels in the tortured cries she hears?
She is no peasant though she loves the fruitful fields;
  She has a heart that smiles on love . . . and yields.
Cretans will back me up—some Cretan speech is true!
  They raised great Jove and claim the praise that's due.   20
(In Crete, the ruler of the star-sown heights of earth
  Drank as a tender suckling fresh from birth.)
Their claims are true; that Jove they raised will testify.
  I'm sure my charges Ceres won't deny.
For at Mt. Ida's foot she saw Iasius hunting   25
  Wild game. His steady hand was not found wanting.
The fatal torch was lit the moment that she looked.
  Love fought it out with Shame, then she was hooked:
Love won the day. Then one could see the furrows dried;
  Crop yields? They barely could be quantified.   30

Instead, when hoes had hoed for all that they were worth,
    And curved shares torn at the unyielding earth;
When seed had scattered equally across the plain;
    Then hopeless farmers vowed their vows in vain.
Great Goddess Ceres found the woods, and lingered where   35
    The braided spikes of wheat fell from her hair.
The only land that had a fruitful year was Crete;
    Where she had stepped, there plenty was replete.
Ida itself, so thick with woods, shone rich in crops
    And wild boars reaped the barley, wheat, and hops.   40
Even King Minos prayed all want lay in the past.
    (He *should* have prayed that Ceres' love would last.)
Blonde Goddess: sleeping by yourself was sad, and so
    On your feast day I have to bear this woe?
Why is that, while *you* get to have your daughter found,   45
    Who rules what Juno can't—life underground?
A holy day should come with women, wine, and song.
    So give *these* to the gods, where they belong.

III.11a

You've hurt me way too long; I won't take any more.
    Love, go away; my heart lies bruised and sore.
It must be true I'm free of you and all your chains;
    I won't bear what I bore: those shameful pains.
I've conquered now, trampling on love like that; I've won,   5
    And now at last my courage has begun.
I'll stay the course and some day reap the benefit
    Of pain. Who knows what good may come of it?
Love, who'd believe I let you chase me from your door,
    A freeman sleeping on the street's hard floor?   10

Could I have slept before your shuttered house, a slave,
 While Whosis took the kisses that you gave?
Worn out, he's sneaked away, wary of the alarms—
 That wounded vet who's had you in his arms.
The only thing that's worse is being seen by him—   15
 A fate for enemies, but twice as grim.
Girl, when did I not stand there proudly at your side,
 Your more-than-patient lover, guard, and guide?
In fact, the folk thought more of you because of me:
 My love made others love you, don't you see?   20
But why retail the lies your tongue has told? Why show
 The oaths you broke to send my soul below?
And should I mention banquets where young men would nod
 As secret signals that your words would prod?
Told she was sick, I ran, in fear for her survival,   25
 Only to find her "healthy" for my rival.
I've borne a lot of this in silence, growing tough.
 Now find some other dupe; I've had enough.
Right now, a votive wreath blesses my vessel's stern;
 She harks to waves, to hear what she may learn.   30
So kill those sweetest nothings that you love to say;
 I'm not the fool that I was yesterday.

III.11b

They pull my heart two ways at once, this love, this hate.
 Love wins; my heart has always been lightweight.
I'll *try* to hate. If not, I'll love against my will.
 (Though oxen hate the yoke, they bear it still.)
I flee your worthlessness; your beauty reels me back.   5
 I know just what you are . . . and what I lack.

I can't live with that body I can't live without—
    A fact that's clear. And so I live in doubt.
If only you were ugly, or you did *some* good;
    Body and soul don't match the way they should.   10
Your face makes for desire, but your deeds, disgrace,
    And in this war, the winner is your face.
By all the laws of love; by all the gods who give
    Themselves to you to be deceived, yet live;
By that fair face those gods formed with the greatest art;   15
    And by your deadly eyes; oh, spare my heart.
Whatever you will be, you will be mine, but choose:
    My willing love or what I can't refuse.
I'd rather see fair winds and have my canvas fill;
    I want to love—not love against my will.   20

III.12

What was that dreadful day you ravens chose to curse
    With caws this constant lover and his verse?
Yes, name the star that I should think rose on my fate.
    What gods are warring with me in their hate?
My one-time love, who started up with only me,   5
    I see is now Rome's common property.
Now, stop me, but I'd swear my books produced her fame.
    And so it is: my Muse spread wide her name.
I earned this! Why did I proclaim her form and face
    Until my verse became her marketplace?   10
My pandering means she pleases louts procured by me.
    Her gate lies open; all the world can see.
So . . . *verse?* I have my doubts; it doesn't do much good
    For me—at least not what I wish it would.

Thebes, Troy, and Caesar wouldn't do, so it would seem;   15
    Corinna's been my Muse's only theme.
The Muses should have left when I began to follow
    This bardic trade—and ditto for Apollo.
But since most people don't believe what most bards say,
    I wish my own light verse had blown away.   20
Poets made: the lock we had Scylla purloin;
    The rabid dogs she wore about her groin;
Winged Mercury; snake-ringleted Medusa's hair;
    Brave Perseus on a horse that flew through air.
We stretched out Titan Tityos in a monstrous space   25
    And stuck three mouths on Cerberus's face.
We gave Enceladus a thousand arms for spears,
    And let the Sirens poison heroes' ears.
Odysseus' wineskin bottled up the eastern wind,
    While Tantalus was racked because he sinned.   30
We ruined Níobe. We gave the Bear its sky,
    Then filled the air with Philomela's cry.
Because of us, love comes in gold, or as a bird,
    Or bull that swims. (Europa, take our word.)
And then there's Proteus, and dragon teeth for seed,   35
    And cattle spewing flame (a fiery breed?).
That Phaethon had sisters weeping amber drips?
    That nymphs were made out of Aeneas' ships?
All ours. We poets wrote of Atreus's meal
    And rocks that heard plucked lyres and could feel.   40
The far-fetched things we think to say, you just can't count.
    Not bound by truth, we are a gushing fount.
Couldn't you see my praise for her was all a lie?
    Then, you believed, and now . . . I long to die.

III.13

Because my wife came from Falisca's orchard town,
    We sought these walls Camillus once brought down.
The priestesses were planning Juno's holy feast:
    Some games; a slaughtered cow (a local beast).
To view those sacred rites was well worthwhile, although   5
    The way was hard and steep, the going slow.
Deep in, there is a grove; the trees are dark and dense.
    One feels divinity, and it's intense.
An altar stone accepts incense and pious prayer—
    A plain stone carved without an artist's care.   10
Here, when the pipe has played its ancient, solemn praise,
    The yearly pomp winds through the covered ways,
And people clap, as rope-led, snow-white heifers pass
    That flourished feeding on Faliscan grass.
Some calves come, too, who have no horns to threaten men,   15
    And one small pig, pulled from the victims' pen.
The alpha ram, its hard brows overhung with horn,
    Goes by, but she-goats earn the goddess' scorn.
(Goat gossip showed the world Queen Juno on the run,
    Stopping the forest flight she had begun.)   20
Even children kill nannies with their spears (child-sized),
    Winning the she-goat "prey" that they have prized.
Where Juno's meant to go, shy girls and boys walk on,
    Sweeping the wide paths where their robes have gone.
The virgins load their curls with gold and glittering gems—   25
    Their gold-clad feet brushed by their pallas' hems—
While like their Greek forebears, veiled in chaste albs of white,
    They balance offerings for the holy rite.
And as the progress swells, the crowd stands hushed in awe.

Juno herself came next (that's what we saw).   30
The rite is Argive: with King Agamemnon dead,
    Halaesus spurned his homeland's wealth and fled
That crime. A refugee, he wandered sea and land
    To raise these walls by his auspicious hand,
Then taught Faliscans Juno's proper liturgy.   35
    May it always bless its folk . . . and me.

III.14

You're beautiful, so I expect you to give in,
    But please don't tell poor me your every sin.
I'm not your censor. You're unchaste, and I'll abide it.
    I'm only asking you to try to hide it.
Saying "I haven't," you haven't—that's what I stress.   5
    They'll call you names *only if you confess.*
So you're insane to trumpet strumpet nights by day,
    Blaring the sins you ought to hide away.
Even the slut who sleeps with any Roman man
    Will bar the eager public if she can.   10
But *you*—you seem to mean to play vile Rumor's snitch,
    Retailing crimes and sins—and which is which.
Re-think your "modesty"; fake what you haven't got.
    I'll go along whether you have or not.
Keep doing what you're doing, but deny you do,   15
    My dear; speak modestly in public, too.
There is a place for guilt; go fill it with delight
    And banish blushing from that pleasure-site.
But once you leave, put all your lewdness off. Instead,
    Go modestly, your love-sins left in bed.   20
Until such time, feel free to let your clothes fall by,

And braid your legs with others, thigh on thigh.
In that place, plunge your hungry tongue through bruisèd lips
    While Venus re-arranges breasts and hips.
Oh, utter every stirring word that you can utter,   25
    Loving until you feel the bed frame shudder.
But after, wear your dress and face with modesty ,
    No sign of loving left for men to see.
Lie to the crowd—and lie to me. Leave me in bliss
    And ignorance—deaf, dumb, and credulous.   30
Why let me see the reams of notes you send to men,
    And on your bed, each place where they have been?
Why show disheveled hair mussed more by love than sleep?
    Who bit your neck and left those marks so deep?
You might as well arraign your faults for me to see;   35
    If you can't spare your name, at least spare me!
My mind goes blank at each confession, and I die,
    Chilled by the blood that I was once warmed by.
That's when I love you, as I *try* to hate the thing
    I love, then pray for what our deaths will bring.   40
I won't give you the third degree or badger you;
    Your lies are good as gifts, and they will do.
But should I stumble on you in your lickerish dark,
    With you a meretrix and I your mark,
Then say I didn't see what I so clearly did;   45
    My eyes will do whatever they are bid.
It's not that hard to conquer those who want to be;
    Just keep "I didn't" in your memory.
That way, when truth alone can't win your wretched case,
    With me for judge, those two words take its place.   50

III.15

My elegies are racing for the finish line,
    So Venus, muse some other verse than mine.
I am Paelignian, and I can rightly say
    These fine songs do that proud in every way.
An heir to ancient, honored men (for what that's worth),   5
    I am no knight by battle, but by birth.
Verona has her favorite son, and Mantua, too;
    I'll be Paelignia's before I'm through.
That land made good the oath of freedom that it swore,
    When Romans feared to fight the Social War.   10
Now, any stranger seeing Sulmo's walls that guard
    Her marshy acres shouldn't find it hard
To say, "That place which makes great poetry, I call
    A land of genius—great however small."
O Venus, Amathusian mother of that scamp,   15
    Remove your golden guidons from my camp.
Lord Bacchus, with his weighty thyrsis, means to force us
    To stronger horses running longer courses.
My peaceful elegies, my gentle Muse, good-bye.
    Let my words live long after I shall die.   20

Ars Amatoria

BOOK I

Let anyone who lacks the art of love read on,
    And having read, his ignorance is gone!
It's art that makes a ship respond to sail and oar,
    And art that drives a team or guides Amor.
Automedon controlled his reins with expert grip,   5
    Like Tiphys, helming that Haemonian ship.
Now Venus says that I'm to rule her tender son;
    I'll be Love's Tiphys and Automedon.
And though he's wild, and far too prone to fight with me,
    He's just a boy; I'll win out easily.   10
(The way that Chiron broke Achilles on a lyre,
    By banking down that youngster's feral fire).
They say that he whom enemies and friends both feared,
    Cowered before a Centaur's hoary beard.
Those hands that Hector felt, Achilles had to hold   15
    Out to the lash; he did as he was told.
Achilles, Love: two pupils. Chiron, me: two teachers.
    Two sons of goddesses, both savage creatures.
The bull endures the yoke; upon his neck it sits.
    And fiery horses clamp down on their bits.   20
So Love succumbs, although his arrow pierce my heart.
    Let him burn his brand or shoot his dart;
The deeper that he wounds, the hotter that wound burns,
    The sooner my revenge pays what he earns.

I will not claim that Phoebus gave me this (my skill),   25
    Or that some high-flown bird has stirred my quill.
I never saw a Clio go, and never saw
    Her sisters fill me with old Hesiod's awe.
No. Life informs these lines, so heed this well-versed bard
    Who sings the truth. O Venus, guide and guard!   30
And stay away, thin ribbons—signs of modesty—
    And flounces hiding feet we mustn't see.
I sing safe, sanctioned love and love affairs in rhyme
    That advocates no *error*, sin, or crime.
First, those of you who come to love as raw recruits   35
    Must find some girl your lover's fancy suits.
Next, work to win the one who pleases you the best.
    Then, make that love endure time's toughest test.
This is my bound, and this my chariot's well-marked ground;
    This is the turnpost it will wheel around.   40

Not yet reined in, footloose and free to roam and run,
    Pick someone you can call "my only one."
She won't come from thin air, straight down from clear blue skies,
    This cynosure of love; you'll need sharp eyes.
The hunter knows just where the stag will find his snare,   45
    And knows the gnashing boar's most likely lair.
Good fowlers know their thickets, and men with a hook
    Know where the fish swim; hence, just where to look.
You, too! Look for substantial love that will go far.
    But first, you need to know where the girls *are*!   50
Now, I won't tell you to go searching with a sail,
    Or send you tramping down some dusty trail.
Perseus got his Andromeda from darkest Ind,
    And Paris went to Greece before he sinned,

But Rome will yield so many pretty girls each day   55
　　　That "Here is all the world" is what you'll say.
Like full Methymnian vines; like massed Gargarian sheaves;
　　　Like teeming fish; like birds amidst the leaves,
Or stars their skies? Far more, the girls who haunt this Rome
　　　The Mother of Aeneas calls her home.   60
If barely blooming beauties set your soul on fire,
　　　Then wait: true virgins couldn't number higher.
If it's young women that you want, a thousand aim
　　　To please—and make you doubt which one to claim.
Perchance your fancy favors older women? Well,   65
　　　Trust me. Mere watching makes their numbers swell!

Just amble under Pompey's portico when Sol
　　　Rides Hercules's lion. Or, go stroll
Where one son gave arcades of marble-cladded stone.
　　　(His mother added riches of her own.)   70
And don't avoid the Empress Livia's gallery.
　　　(So many forbears hanging there to see.)
Apollo's temple, too, where Belus' daughters stand.
　　　(They kill their men; he threatens, sword in hand.)
Adonis, mourned by Venus, also has a shrine,   75
　　　And Jewish sites of worship work just fine.
Don't write off Io's temple, either; linen-wrapped,
　　　Jove's heifer draws them till, like her, they're trapped.
Even the courts (would you believe it?) suit Love's sports—
　　　His torches burning in the heated torts.   80
Where just below her marble temple—Venus' shrine—
　　　The Appian fountain's leaping waters shine,
There, often in that place, some counselor gets caught
　　　(Who thought for others, gives himself no thought).

There, often in that place, he finds, beyond belief,   85
    He's speechless—and his next case is *his* brief.
There Venus in her nearby temple laughs at one
    Who pled for hire. Now, *his* case has begun!

But theatres are best, where seats curve up in layers;
    These places set the scene for answered prayers.   90
You'll find there one to love, or one to only play with;
    Someone to sample, or someone to stay with.
An ant will come and go all day, in endless lines,
    Bearing the grains on which it usually dines.
A bumblebee will stumble on some flowered dell,   95
    Then hover there in thyme's sweetmeadow smell.
Well that's how all the smartest women crowd the shows
    In numbers, till my faltering judgment goes.
Where they are able to be seen, they come to see—
    A place that's lethal to all chastity.   100

Romulus, you made these shows trouble, way back when
    The Sabine rapes consoled Rome's wifeless men.
Back then, no awnings shaded marble seats; the play
    Went on without our rosy saffron spray.
There, leafy fronds the Palatine had borne were scattered   105
    About; simplicity was all that mattered.
The people sat on steps of turf, shading their hair
    With broad and random leaves found growing there.
Each looked around, eyeing the girls that he preferred,
    And in his silent heart was deeply stirred.   110
Then, as the Tuscan flautist made a simple sound,
    And dancers triple-stamped the beaten ground,
And rough men clapped (their taste had not yet been refined),

The king gave them the sign for which they pined.
At once, they jumped up, clamor making passion clear, 115
 And virgin-hungry hands made virgins fear.
As far-too-timid, eagle-fearing pigeons fly;
 As spring lambs run from wolves (it's live or die);
Just so, those virgins feared the men who made a rush.
 No virgin now retained her maiden blush. 120
Their fear was one, but didn't wear one fearful face:
 Some tore their hair; some stared off into space.
Some shut down in their shock; some cried out for their mothers.
 One runs; another stays. One wails; another's
Dazed by it all. But all get led off, spoils or prey. 125
 Their fear made many pretty in a way.
If any fought, or in such fight were even bolder,
 The lust-filled man threw her over his shoulder,
Saying, "Why spoil your tender eyes with tears? I'll be
 A husband like your mother's was, you see?" 130
Romulus, you knew how to pay your soldiers right;
 Pay *me* that way and I'll enlist tonight!
Clearly, from that our current playhouse mores came . . .
 A trap for beauties stage shows still remain.

Remember gallant horses, too (I mean the races): 135
 The Circus has so many useful places,
With no necessity for secret-signaling hands,
 Or nods that tell you that she understands.
Just sit beside her; it's the open-seating plan,
 So nudge against her thigh the best you can. 140
Like it or not, the seats mean closeness, and that's good;
 Tight spaces leave you touching where you should.
Look for an opening for harmless social chat,

Starting with public words (what's wrong with that?).
Ask earnestly whose horses now are coming in,   145
    Then quickly back her favorites to win.
And when the ivory parade of gods goes by,
    Clap loud for Lady Venus—don't be shy.
Say that a speck of dust should fall into her lap;
    Flick it away with a quick finger-snap.   150
If nothing's there, then flick that nothing anyway.
    Find any old excuse, then . . . seize the day!
And if her hem should hang, dragging the ground a bit,
    Save earth and hem by neatly lifting it.
This wins a prize (if she permits): you get the chance   155
    To give her legs a momentary glance.
There's more: be sure you know whose knees those are one row
    Behind: her soft back *isn't* where they go.
The simple mind will find delight in trifles: much
    May come from cushions lent an artful touch.   160
Also, a little fan can help to keep her cool;
    Then prop her tender feet up with a stool.

Yes, look at all the Circus offers . . . and the Forum—
    Whose wretched floor can also draw a quorum.
For Love has often battled on its bloody sands,   165
    Inflicting wounds on those safe in the stands.
He asks to see a program, touches what's inviting,
    Chit-chats, and bets . . . not knowing which man's fighting.
And then . . . Love's arrow. Deeply wounded, he
    Becomes like victims that he's come to see.   170

And didn't Caesar re-enact that sea-fight (when
    The Greeks and Persians fought)? That's when young men

And girls came flocking into Rome. From coast to coast
    They came, till all the world called Rome its host.
Who didn't find some love in all that surging mass?   175
    How many fell for foreign girls—alas!

See now how Caesar looks to add what empire lacks:
    The far Far East will soon enjoy our Pax.
Parthia, you'll pay, while buried Crassi shall exult.
    Our eagles rise you thought you could insult.   180
"Vengeance is here," young Gaius cries. And so, no more
    A boy, he goes to wage a grown man's war.
Stop counting birthdays of the gods, you cowards, you!
    Caesars show courage long before they're due.
Great god-like power comes faster than the years can bring,   185
    And thinks delay a damned ignoble thing.
Tirynthian Hercules crushed snakes barehanded when
    A tot, already Jove-like even then.
Bacchus, a boy still, *how* big were you when you bashed
    Down India with your wand that smote and smashed?   190
Gaius, you have your father's age and power; now wage
    This war . . . and win it with that power and age.
This kind of war is what a Caesar fights, O bold
    Young Prince of Youths (and one day, of the old).
Avenge these brothers' wounds; you've brothers of your own.   195
    A son yourself, defend a father's throne.
Your father—father of your country—arms you now;
    Your foes attacked their sire, who would not bow.
You'll carry pious pikes, they'll shoot their shameful darts;
    Your eagles all will stand by righteous hearts.   200
The Parthians' cause is lost; then let them lose by war.
    My Prince, add eastern wealth to Latium's store!

Our fathers, Mars and Caesar: lend him all your power
    (One god and one god-at-some-future-hour).
Listen! Gaius will conquer and I'll sing those deeds   205
    To glorify his name as time recedes.
Oh, you will stand, and with my words, exhort your men,
    Gaius. I pray they may not fail you then.
My verse will be of Roman fronts and Parthian backs—
    Cowards who fire from horses making tracks.   210
What's left in your defeat if you "retreat to win"?
    O Parthian, that's a bad way to begin.
So there will come a day when Gaius, shining bright,
    Rides golden with his four-horse team in white.
Then, Parthian chiefs will stagger on, necks bowed by chains.   215
    They'll never flee again across the plains.
That day, young joyous men and girls will revel so,
    Their celebrating hearts will overflow.
"What peak is that?" she'll ask. "What land?" "What king of note?"
    "What stream's personified up on that float?"   220
Tell her everything, and not just if you're bid;
    If you don't know, respond as if you did:
"This one's Euphrates, wreathed with reeds; and that one there
    Is Tigris with the deep-blue, dripping hair.
These are Armenians. Those? They're Persians, from the race   225
    Of Danaë. That? Some quaint Parthian place."
Each one will be some chief; give him his proper name—
    Or not. If you don't know, it's all the same.

A banquet means an opening; with table set,
    There's something more than wine that you can get!   230
There, wine-dark Love draws Bacchus to his tender arms
    To hug the drugged god's horns and other charms.
When wine has soaked through Cupid's thirsty wings, he stays,

And stands stock-still (how heavily wine weighs!).
But soon enough he shakes his pinions dry, and hearts   235
    He barely sprinkles feel his wounding darts.
Wine leads us on and sets us up; our passions flare.
    It drowns all sorrows, till there's no more care.
Then laughter comes; then even paupers grow assured.
    Then wrinkles melt; the deepest wound is cured.   240
Then rare simplicity appears; unlocks the mind.
    For drink means artfulness is left behind.
At times like these, girl huntresses have caught their game
    (Venus *in vino*: fire in the flame).
At times like those, don't credit late-night lamps—
                    they're treacherous.   245
    (Night wine will dim your judgment when
                     you're lecherous.)
When Paris said to Venus, "Goddess, you outdo
    These two," he needed daylight. You will, too.
The night hides blemishes; defects are all excused.
    By midnight not a girl ever looks used.   250
Use daylight judging gems, or fine, maroon-dyed wool;
    Daylight will tell you if she's beautiful.

But why this list of hunting grounds where girls resort?
    Why count them, like the sands? The time's too short.
The same for Baiae by the Bay, all laced with sails   255
    (And hot springs that the thermal sulfur veils).
Someone returning from there, heart-pierced, said,
    "Say! Those aren't 'healthy' springs; I've been misled!"
Then there's a grove just out of town—Diana's shrine—
    Whose slave-priests kill to be the next in line.   260
She's virgin, so Diana, who hates Cupid's darts,
    Has wounded—will keep wounding—human hearts.

So far, my Muse, riding on mis-matched wheels, has shown
    You where to snare a lover of your own.
Hard as it is, I'll try to tell you how to seize her,   265
    And harder still, the art of how to please her.
Men everywhere, pay heed; and may the common run
    Of men applaud this work that I've begun.

First, rest assured there is no woman you can't get;
    But keep in mind, you have to spread your net!   270
Spring birds will sing no more, cicadas make no sound,
    And rabbits run Arcadian hounds to ground
Before well-tempted women won't succumb to skill;
    Even the ones you think unwilling, will.
Men love to love in secret; so do women, gladly   275
    Disguising their desires (men do that badly).
If only asking first weren't something men were used to.
    Soon, that's what conquered girls would be reduced to.
In meadows, heifers moo so bulls can see they're moved.
    Mares whinny to their stallions horny-hooved.   280
We passionate men love with a less-than-frantic soul,
    Keeping those fires well under our control.

Take Byblis' brother-love: should that be bothered with?
    At least she hanged herself (so says the myth).
There's Myrrha, too, loving her sire indecently—   285
    And now confined inside an ambering tree.
She weeps away her name, anointing us with myrrh;
    We're chrism'd by the tears that fall from her.
There was a white bull once, where Ida's woods conferred
    Their shade upon that glory of the herd.   290
Between his horns, a spot that barely could be spied—

His one black mark. The rest was milk-white hide.
Oh, how Cydonia's heifers on the isle of Crete
    (And in Cnossus) longed to bear his weight.
Pasiphaë rejoiced at what he could arouse;   295
    Jealous, she hated all those pretty cows.
(I sing a truth Crete's hundred towns cannot deny,
    No matter how those lying Cretans try).
To feed that lord, she'd pick the sweetest grasses growing—
    The tenderest leaves she hoped would set him lowing—   300
Then wander with the herd. Nor was she slow in going
    Because her human husband lived; his overthrowing
Was by a bull! O girl, what good are gowns when you
    Pursue a bovine lord? What can *they* do?
And why a mirror here, where hillside cattle stray?   305
    Why rearrange your hair five times a day?
Believe instead the glass that says you're not a cow.
    Oh, how you've wished for horns to crown that brow!
But think of Minos; why begin some mad beguine?
    At least pick out a *man*; don't be obscene.   310
Spurning her bed, the queen begins to haunt the fields,
    A kind of Maenad, maddened till she yields.
How often did she scowl when she beheld a cow,
    And think, "How *could* this *thing* delight him? *How?*
Look how she flaunts herself there in the grass,   315
    With 'charms' she thinks no heifer could surpass."
No sooner said than heifers would be led away,
    Poor innocents, to learn what oxbows weigh.
Or else she'd have her rival butchered ("God commands!"),
    To hold the entrails in her joyous hands.   320
She held such innards often (gods must be appeased),
    Taunting, "Go *now* and see if my lord's pleased!"

Europa first, then Io, is Pasiphaë—
    A heifer and a girl bull-borne to sea.
And yet that prize bull filled her (hidden in a crate);   325
    The offspring proved just who had been her mate.
If Aerope had left Thyestes all alone
    (Could that be hard—to make one man your own?),
The god would not have turned his horses back at noon,
    To drive toward Dawn when it was far too soon.   330
And Nisus' daughter cut his purple lock, and so
    Got all wrapped up in rabid dogs below.
And Agamemnon, fleeing Neptune for his life
    (And Mars, by land), fell victim to his wife.
Who has not mourned Creusa, burnt in Ephyre?   335
    The children cruel Medea thought to slay?
Amyntor's Phoenix, from his gouged-out sockets, cried;
    Hippolytus was torn by horses terrified.
Phineus, you blinded guiltless sons, only to pay:
    You yielded up *your* eyes the self-same way.   340
And female lust caused all these crimes! Men are more mild,
    Women more prone to let desire run wild.

So there! You *can* get women that you want. Not one
    Percent will say no to the work you've done.
But yes or no, girls love to hear the hopeful male   345
    Who asks. And what's the harm if you should fail?
"If you should fail"? But *why?* We all love fresh, new flings.
    The flesh is weak . . . and wants its neighbor's things.
In someone else's field, the grass is always greener,
    The udders on our own cows always leaner.   350

First, cultivate your love's coiffeuse, for with her aid,
 You'll smooth your entrée to the choice you've made.
Be sure she's privy to your mistress' thoughts and cares,
 And circumspect with all your love's affairs.
Corrupt this lady's maid with promises and prayers.   355
 (Your love-success depends on what she shares.)
She'll choose the time (the choice a doctor's always making)
 Her lady's heart is ripest for the taking.
She's ripest for that taking when she's full of life—
 A fertile field where golden grain grows rife.   360
The heart set free by grief lies open; that's the heart
 That waits for Venus's seductive art.
Troy wept in gloom defending what was dear by force
 Of arms, but leapt for joy to have that horse!
So try her when she's rival-wounded; watch her sob,   365
 Then see she gets revenge. Make it your job.
The morning maid who combs her hair can urge her, too.
 (Why not see what sail *and* oar can do?)
After a heartfelt little sigh, the maid should say,
 "I guess there's just no way to make *him* pay."   370
Then have her talk you up with hints and suasive praises:
 You're "mad"! Insane! A love that burns and blazes!
Move fast, before sails droop and breezes blow away;
 Like brittle ice, wrath melts when you delay.
What's that you ask? Seduce the maid herself? Think twice   375
 About the risk before you roll *those* dice.
Love makes some girls slow go-betweens, some fast. One pleads
 Your case; the other tries to fill *her* needs.
There's risk no matter what. I *know*: "no risk, no gain."
 But if you want my best advice, abstain.   380
(Come follow me; I'll show you all the easy way—

No mountain trails to lead young men astray.)
All right: suppose, in playing messenger, her figure
    Should please you no less than her helpful vigor.
Master the mistress first, and *then* the maid. The maid   385
    Is *never* where to start some escapade.
And one more thing: if you believe my art and me,
    And jealous winds don't blow my words to sea:
Either *don't try* . . . or else *be sure.* That way, she can't
    Inform on you; she's a participant!   390
The bird that's limed is trapped, no matter how it flaps;
    The boar goes nowhere when the nets collapse.
The fish that's taken by the sneaky hook's undone;
    Once you've begun, don't leave until you've won.
So, sharing in your little sin, she'll be discreet,   395
    Your knowledge of your mistress' mind complete.
But don't let on! The maid's affairs must not be known.
    You'll know your darling's thoughts just like your own.

If you think only sailors note the seasons, think again,
    For farmers watch as well for likely rain.   400
The earth won't let you cast your seed just when you please;
    Don't launch a ship at random on green seas.
The same with tender girls: not every day's the best
    For love; some times are better than the rest.
If it's her birthday, or those special Kalends when   405
    Venus and Mars will rendezvous again;
If trinkets in the Circus aren't on sale (the way
    They were), but only jewels on display;
Defer your plans. That's when bad storms are set in motion.
    Pleiads threaten? The Kid drowns in the ocean?   410
Hold off. Sailing such seas, you won't get very far,

But end up clinging to some splintered spar.
You might as well begin the day the Allia's flood
    Is running red with wounded Latians' blood.
Or even worse, that seventh day come round once more   415
    That Hebrew worship is intended for.
Avoid her birthday! Pass it by and don't look back;
    Whatever day requires gifts is black!
Succeed, and still they'll have their way. Girls *will* discover
    The artful means to fleece an eager lover.   420
If Missy's in a buying mood, you know some tout
    Will tempt her while you're sitting by, shut out.
She's cunning: "Darling, lend me your judicious eye."
    Next comes the kiss—and then you're asked to buy.
She swears that it will give her years of sheer delight.   425
    She's "got" to have it, since "the price is right."
Plead lack of cash, she'll take your note. Give up the fight—
    And curse the day you ever learned to write.
How can she claim a birthday cake five times a year?
    Who would have thought that birthdays came so near?   430
What do you do when she pretends her dear friend's died?
    She's lost an earring! All last night, she cried.
So many things you'll never see again, girls "borrow,"
    But they don't care; you "lend" things to your sorrow.
Ten months, ten tongues, and still they wouldn't be enough   435
    To tell of women's ruses—not by *half*.

Let letter-tablet wax go first; it may convey
    The eloquence of what you're trying to say.
Let wax words and endearments dear to lovers go;
    Whoever you may be, your prayers should flow.   440
Achilles, touched by pleas, gave Priam back his son;

By praying voices, vengeful gods are won.
　　Make promises! They do no harm, so who can chide us?
　　　　In promises, each man can be a Midas.
Just once have faith in Hope, and she'll have faith in you—   445
　　　　A cheater, but . . . a useful goddess, too.
The trouble is, you give, and she no longer heeds you;
　　　　She loses nothing and no longer needs you.
Give nothing; always seem about to be a donor.
　　　　Many a barren field has duped its owner.   450
The gambler goes on losing so he *won't* have lost.
　　　　The dice entice the hand from which they're tossed.
"This is the task; this is the work": gift-free success.
　　　　To save what's given, she'll give more, not less!
So scratch a billet-doux, then send it off to sound   455
　　　　Her out (and be the first to tread that ground).
Cydippe tricked herself when, unawares, she read
　　　　Aloud, repeating what an apple said.

Roman young men, learn your trade; the liberal arts
　　　　Aren't just for calming clients' trembling hearts.   460
As judge, or populace, or Senate yields to you,
　　　　So eloquence will win a woman, too.
But hide your art: don't play the highbrow. Try, instead,
　　　　To let your language show you're not well read.
Only a dolt would send his girl some stuffed oration.   465
　　　　(Back come curt letters in reciprocation.)
Plain, ordinary words create a sense of trust,
　　　　As if you're there. But coaxing's still a must.
She sends your letter back, unread? Don't sit and mope,
　　　　But persevere—and never give up hope.   470
In time, unwilling cattle plough without a fight;

The filly's taught to feel the bit is right.
An iron ring thins down from constant wear and tear,
    And constantly the ground grinds down the share.
What's harder than a rock? What's softer than a wave?   475
    Still, gentle water hollows out the cave.
Hard work *could* win Penelope (well, who can tell?);
    We know that Troy fell late—and yet it fell.
She's read your blandishments but won't send back *her* note?
    Don't fret. At least she read the words you wrote.   480
Whoever wants to read will write back in the end.
    It's bit-by-bit on which you can depend.
At first, some sullen note may "beg you to desist";
    She may write back, "You really must resist."
In truth, she fears you *will*, while hoping that you won't.   485
    Go on! You'll never win her if you don't.

Meanwhile, if she is being carried on her chair,
    Disguise your sidling up, and take care,
If someone's there—don't let yourselves be overheard;
    With two-faced words, your meaning can be blurred.   490
Or if her aimless feet go wandering some arcade,
    Contrive a friendly dalliance in its shade.
And as you walk, sometimes go slow, sometimes move fast;
    Sometimes go first and sometimes follow last.
Don't be afraid to slip between the columns, glide   495
    Around, or end up nicely side by side.
Don't let her sit in theatres alone, but go . . .
    And view her more-than-lovely cameo.
It's fine to look, but finer to appreciate.
    (There's much a gesture, much a brow, can state.)   500
Clap when some mincing dancer mimes the ingenue;

Applaud whoever plays the lover, too.
If she gets up, get up; and if she sits, you sit.
    Your time is hers; her wish is wasting it.

I don't advise a curling iron for your hair,   505
    Or pumicing your legs until they're bare.
That's for the Magna Mater singers, chanting odes
    Or ululating in the Phrygian modes.
For men, slight grooming's best; when Theseus won the fair
    Ariadne, no pin or clip held back his hair.   510
Unkempt Hippolytus won Phaedra; Myrrha's boy,
    Adonis, forest-born, was Venus' joy.
Plain cleanliness works best, and drill-field tans don't hurt.
    Your well-cut toga should be free of dirt.
Keep shoe straps loose and buckles bright—no rust.   515
    (But don't forget that good fit's still a must.)
Be sure a barber, not a butcher, cuts your hair
    And trims your beard with care. Please try to wear
Nails short and clean. Be sure no ugly hair growth shows,
    Sprouting from the hollows of your nose.   520
Don't let your breath go sour, and you should take note:
    Armpits must never smell like billy goat.
But any more than that, let wanton girls employ—
    Or any man who would prefer a boy.

Now Liber calls his bard; he helps keep love alive.   525
    The flame with which *he* burns, he wants to thrive.
Crazed Ariadne, wandering down the alien shore
    Of little Dia, where the waters roar,
Came fresh from having wakened—barefoot, loosely gowned,
    Disoriented, blonde hair all unbound.   530

She cried out Theseus' name. The sea was deaf and dumb,
 As down soft cheeks, the tears began to come.
She cried out and she cried, and both became her well,
 Making her charming as the teardrops fell.
Fists beat against her tender breasts repeatedly: 535
 "That traitor's gone. What will become of me?
What will become of me?" she cried. Then . . . cymbals crashed!
 And everywhere, the thundering drums were bashed.
Her cry half-cried, she fainted from her fear and lay
 As pale as if her blood had drained away.   540
Then . . . look! The Bacchants, hair blown back. Again, behold!
 His harbingers, the Satyrs, wild and bold.
Behold that sot Silenus on his swaybacked ass,
 Grasping its mane, about to hit the grass.
He's after Bacchants, who re-group and circle back. 545
 No horseman he, he gives the ass a thwack,
Then tumbles off old Long-Ears, landing on his head.
 "Dad, get up!" cry the Satyrs. "You're not dead!"
Then Bacchus, in a chariot grape vines enfold,
 Arrived. His tigers' reins were made of gold. 550
Her voice, her color, and all thoughts of Theseus fled.
 Three times she tried to flee, but stopped, in dread.
A shaken, slender reed, she shuddered in her fears—
 A slight cane, trembling in the marshy meres.
And Bacchus said, "I'm here, and I will care for you. 555
 Don't fear. I'll do what Theseus couldn't do.
You'll be a constellation—such your gift shall be.
 The Cretan Crown, you'll guide ships lost at sea."
He speaks, and lest she fear the beasts, he leaps, and lands
 With pressing feet upon the Dian sands. 560
He caught her to him (she was weak), then off they drove.

(It isn't hard when you're the son of Jove.)
Some sang, "Euhoe"; some "Hail, Hymenaeus," said.
    Then bride and god meet on the sacred bed.

So when the Dionysian gifts come round to you,   565
    And some girl shares *your* couch, here's what to do:
Beg the Nyctelian spirits not to let the red
    Wine hurt your flirting with a foggy head.
Here, you can say so much, from which she may infer
    Your ambiguities were meant for her.   570
In pale wine, write sweet nothings—all that you are able;
    She'll "read" that she's your mistress on this table.
Look deep into her eyes with eyes that seem on fire;
    A silent look can speak of great desire.
Be sure to be the first to touch the cup her lip   575
    Has touched; where she drank, that's where you should sip.
Whatever food that girl has fiddled with or fingered,
    Ask for; be sure your hand on hers has lingered.
And try to please your woman's spouse; make that your end.
    He could become quite useful as a friend.   580
Drinking by lot, concede your place, your drinking crown;
    Give him your turn by turning your turn down.
Sitting below (or with you), he should eat before you.
    Be sure to let him talk first, though he bore you.
The broad highway? To call yourself a friend, but cheat.   585
    The broad highway is sinning's easy street.
Some agents act in more than you may bargain for,
    Watching not just their charges, but far more.

How much to drink? The right amount is not quite to
    Where mind—and feet—can't do what they must do.   590

Whenever nasty quarrels fuelled by wine begin,
  Be sure you keep *your* fists from joining in.
Eurytion, soaked in wine, was cut down at a stroke.
  At drinking banquets, tell a friendly joke.
Sing—if you can; and if your arms are supple, dance.   595
  If you've got talents, please at every chance.
Real drunkenness can harm, but sometimes, if you fake it—
  Your clever tongue as thick as you can make it—
The world will put down what you say to too much wine,
  When what you say or do has "crossed the line."   600
Try this: "The lady's health!" Then, "Health to her bed mate,"
  While silent thoughts of him are filled with hate.
And when the board's been cleared, and guests are streaming out,
  You'll get the chance you need in all that rout.
Join it! Inch up on her as she's departing. Catch   605
  Her sleeve, and try to make your footsteps match.
The time to talk is now; don't be some bashful farmer;
  (Venus, like Chance, will favor the brave charmer).
Don't let your smooth talk yield to poets' rules; have just
  One goal, and talk will come from this self-trust.   610
Become The Lover; tell her that your heart is aching.
  (The tactics have to be of your own making.)
But that's not hard; all women *know* men want them madly.
  Even the ugliest believe this gladly.
Of course, mock lovers often start to love for real,   615
  And end up feeling what they've claimed to feel!
Girls, don't be hard on phony lovers, actors who
  Deceive; today's false love may yet turn true.
The time is now for flattering words to catch her soul—
  Streams undercutting banks as waters roll.   620
And don't stop praising her—her face; her lovely hair;

Her dainty feet; her hands beyond compare.
Even a chaste girl loves to hear you praise her face,
    And virgins find their beauty full of grace.
Why else would Juno and Minerva be mad yet   625
    About that prize at Troy they didn't get?
The bird of Juno, when he's praised, will spread his tail
    Of riches; silence is to no avail.
Even at busy courses, hurried horses savor
    A neck rub and a comb that curries favor.   630

Promise girls anything that works, and don't be shy
    At calling on some god to testify.
For Jove on high just laughs at lovers' perjuries,
    Telling the winds, "Blow them across the seas!"
Jove used to swear to Juno falsely, by the Styx,   635
    So now he favors those who play his tricks.
It helps to say the gods exist. Let's take that line,
    And give old hearths their incense and their wine.
The gods don't "sleep" in something like a lack of care;
    Believe. Live piously. The gods are there.   640
Don't steal from friends, but keep your word. Show piety,
    Avoid all fraud, and keep your hands blood-free.
But if you're smart, cheat only girls and have your fun.
    Allow yourself this fraud, but just this one.
Yes, cheat the cheaters; most of them are far from good.   645
    Catch them in their own traps—it's right you should!
They say that Egypt had no rain for nine long years,
    And all that blessed it were the people's tears.
When Thrasius told Busiris Jove could be appeased,
    But only by a stranger's blood, that pleased   650
Busiris, who replied, "Then you shall be Jove's first

Victim—a stranger slaking Egypt's thirst."
And in Perillus' bull, Phalaris had him burned;
    He was its victim, in a death he'd earned.
Both kings were just: no fairer law in all the land   655
    Than that death-dealers die by what they've planned.
Therefore, so perjured women rightly may be tricked,
    Give them the wound they taught us to inflict.

Tears help as well; tears melt life's adamantine peaks.
    So show her, if you can, your tear-drenched cheeks.   660
If tears won't come (and sometimes they just don't), then why
    Not wipe a sweat-damp hand across your eye?
What truly wise man won't have kissed her and cajoled?
    And if you must, take what she would withhold!
Perhaps at first she'll fight, and call you wicked, though   665
    She really wants to lose to such a foe.
Be careful not to bruise her tender lips; too rough,
    And she can claim that you weren't soft enough.
But men who do receive such kisses but ignore
    "The rest," won't merit kisses any more.   670
So after kissing, much was missing still? Oh, dear!
    Sheer bumpkin bumbling, not shy shame or fear.
It's all right using force: girls like it. Often, they
    Will *want* to yield what they won't give away.
Some women take delight in brute assaults; they act   675
    As if it's quite a coup to be attacked.
And longed-for women who escape and call you cad?
    Their faces fake their joy; they're *really* sad.
Take Phoebe's and her sister's rapist: neither picked him,
    Though each was more than happy as a victim.   680
Achilles and the girl from Scyros are well known,

Their tale worth telling for the moral shown.
Venus, her beauty praised, had fixed the fatal prize
    And bested two where Ida's piedmont lies.
And from Achaia there had come to live in Troy   685
    That Helen who had wed with Priam's boy.
But Greeks were swearing fealty to the injured spouse—
    Public support for his dishonored house.
Achilles, if he hadn't heard his mother's prayers,
    Wouldn't have basely worn what woman wears.   690
What's this, Achilles? Spinning wool? That's not your game.
    Athena's other art will win you fame.
A *basket*, boy? That arm should bear a shield instead.
    Your yarn-filled hand will cut Prince Hector dead.
The distaff wound about with yarn is for some maid;   695
    Your spear-hand should be brandishing a blade.
A virgin princess shared his room, but what escaped her
    Revealed itself at last as male: he raped her.
So yes, it's true that she was conquered by brute force,
    But that's what she'd been wishing for, of course.   700
She begged him, "Stay," as he was rushing off, the spindle
    Discarded; now it's war he means to kindle.
So where's the "violence"? Why cling to someone who
    "Defiled" you? Why sweet words that bill and coo?
Now in the same way that it's shameful to begin,   705
    When others start, there's fun in giving in.
He's far too sure of his own charms if he expects
    To see the first move from the fairer sex.
With wheedling words, let men ask first; that way,
    She'll welcome coaxing words he comes to say.   710
To get her, ask! That's all she's waiting for. So ply her
    With all the whys and whens of your desire.

It's Jupiter who asked the heroines of old;
 No girl seduced him; who'd have been so bold?
When sensing your pursuit has puffed her with conceit,   715
 Break off awhile, sounding a brief retreat.
Women *will* chase what's hard to get, spurning what's rash,
 So ease her burden: don't be quite so brash.
No need to make your hope of her too clear by too
 Much asking; posing as "a friend" will do.   720
(I've seen some straightlaced girls deluded by this "friend."
 The worshipper turns lover in the end.)

A pale complexion's bad in sailors, who should be
 Tanned from the sun and weathered by the sea.
The same for farmers always ploughing up their furrows,   725
 Raking the soil, and smoothing out with harrows.
You athletes, too, who struggle for the olive crown,
 Should be embarrassed if your skin's not brown.
But lovers should be pale; a whiter shade's the best
 For looks—a truth that only fools contest.   730
Orion, pale for Side, wandered in the wood;
 Pale Daphnis' Naiad left him where he stood.
Lean bodies show true feeling. And it's always good
 To hide your glistening hair beneath a hood.
Long lovers' vigils thin their bodies; so do care   735
 And worry born of some great love affair.
To win your heart's desire, look miserable. That way,
 "This man's in love," observers all will say.
Should I complain—or warn—that right and wrong's the same?
 Friendship's a name, and trust an *empty* name.   740
If you're in love, telling your friend's not smart. He'll hear
 You praise her; *then* guess what you'll have to fear.

Perhaps you'll say, "Patroclus kept Achilles' trust,
    And Phaedra—with Pirithous—was just.
Pylades loved Hermione the way a god   745
    Loved Pallas, Castor Helen: nothing odd."
If *that's* your hope, then apples grow on tamarisk trees,
    And river-wading gets you honeybees.
The shameful pleases; selfish pleasure's what's enjoyed—
    Especially if the pleasure's schadenfreude.   750
The shame! No rival has to be a lover's fear.
    If you'd be safe, avoid your faithful peer.
Don't trust your brother, cousin, or your dearest friend;
    They'll make you fear and worry without end.

I meant to stop, but girls' hearts vary by the score,   755
    You'll need at least as many ploys . . . or more.
The same earth can't grow everything; one soil's for wine,
    And one for olives. Elsewhere, wheat does fine.
Like countless faces are the kinds of all those hearts;
    Wise men must play as many countless parts,   760
Now Proteus, in turning into ocean foam,
    Now boars, or trees, or lions. Fish come home
In nets sometimes, and sometimes only hooks will do;
    Occasionally, you have to spear them through.
Don't make one method fit all ages; older deer   765
    Will spot your snares far off, and not come near.
Don't shock the prude, and highbrows leave the dull nonplussed.
    Both types at once will fill with self-disgust.
So, it happens: afraid to love an honest man,
    Girls take the most unsuitable they can.   770

One part is done; two parts remain, like fore and aft;
    The anchor drops to hold my modest craft.

BOOK II

In triumph now, cry out "Hurray!" and then "Hurray!"
    Again. My nets have snagged their fallen prey.
The happy lover gives a fresh palm to my verse
    And finds old Hesiod's and Homer's worse!
That's how the stranger Paris took both wife and flight   5
    From fierce Amyclae; how his sails shone bright!
Hippodamia, that's like your Pelops (how scary it
    Must have been when snatched by alien chariot).
Hey, what's the rush, young man? Our ship's still far from port,
    On a journey anything but short.   10
It's not enough my verse got you her loving heart;
    Art won her, and to *keep* her you'll need art
As well. It's easier to get than hold and guard.
    One rests on luck; the other task is hard.
Oh, now if ever, Venus, favor me. Your son   15
    And Erato—their names of love are one.
I have great schemes! That boy Amor? I plan to say
    What arts will make that errant wanderer stay.
He's flighty, and he has two wings to fly away;
    It's hard to make him—or those wings—obey.   20

Take Minos, blocking all escape routes for his "guest" . . .
    Who with his daring feathers passed that test.
When Daedalus had locked him in—that mother's sin
    (Where bull-man stopped, a man-bull would begin)—
He said, "Conclude my exile, Minos. You are just;   25

I beg you: let my homeland have my dust.
A harsh fate harried me from home, and that is why
    I couldn't live there; let me go and die.
If I have failed you, please just let my boy go free,
    But if you won't, have mercy then on me."   30
These words he spoke, and would have spoken more than these,
    But still the king denied him his release.
When Daedalus heard, he cried out, "Now, O Daedalus, now!
    If you're so damned ingenious, show us how.
King Minos holds the land; King Minos has the sea.   35
    By earth or water, we will not get free.
One way is left: the sky; the sky, then, we shall try.
    Forgive my plan, O Jupiter Most High.
Great king, I do not mean to touch your starry throne;
    One path is left, and it is this alone.   40
We'd swim back through the Styx, were there some Stygian route.
    Man needs new laws; I'll make him laws to suit."
Need breeds invention now; who would have thought that man
    Could travel through the air? And yet he can.
So Daedalus prepared his "oars": he tied together,   45
    With threads of linen, feather after feather,
Fitting them all, with softened wax, against a frame.
    Soon, Daedalus achieved his wondrous aim.
His glad son touched the wings. That they had been designed
    For him to wear never entered his mind.   50
"These are the 'ships' for home, the aids we must employ
    Fleeing Minos," the father told his boy.
"Minos can't close the sky, just land and sea. Cut through
    The air on waxen wings; this you can do.
But do not take your bearings by a flight path toward   55
    The Virgin Bear, or by Orion's sword.

Take up your wings and follow me, for I shall lead,
    And you will be protected. But, take heed!
For if we fly too aether-high, too near the sun,
    Then melting wax will mean we've come undone.   60
And if we fly too low, winging our wave-crest way,
    Light feathers will grow heavy with the spray.
So let your sails respect the wind that fills them, son;
    The high and low are courses you must shun."
He rigs the boy's gear, teaching while he speaks these words,   65
    The way their mother teaches newborn birds.
And then the wings he's made, he fits upon his back,
    Shifting their weight to split the scudding wrack.
Now poised for flight, he's kissed his son, but cannot speak
    The words; a father's tears run down his cheek.   70
Above the flat fields rose a hill no mountain's height,
    From which they launched their bodies' fatal flight.
Now as he works his own wings, Daedalus looks back
    To watch his son's; the father stays on track,
Delighting in the wondrous voyage. Free of fear,   75
    The boy flies high, with daring art, too near
The sun. Meanwhile, the pair is seen: an angler stops
    And stares, scared stiffer than the pole he drops.
With Samos on the left (and Delos quickly gone,
    And Naxos gone, and Paros) they fly on,   80
Lebinthos on the right, and cool Calymne's trees.
    They passed rich Astypalaea's fish-filled seas.
Then . . . bold youth stirred that boy. Too reckless in the sky,
    He left his father and he flew too high.
His straps and struts collapse, wax melting near the sun.   85
    Those arms flap thinnest air; he comes undone.

Now heaven-high, he sees the sea that terrifies;
    In panic-fear, the darkness fills his eyes.
The wax runs down; with naked arms, he shakes and flails,
    Shuddering. Buoyant aether quickly fails.   90
He falls, and calls out, "Father! Oh, I'm swept away!"
    The green waves stopped the words he choked to say.
Poor father (now no father)! "Icarus!" his cry,
    His fear exclaims, "My son! Where do you fly?"
Seeing the floating wings, he cries the same.   95
    Earth keeps those bones; that sea now bears the name.

Minos couldn't clip the wings of one mere man;
    To check a little wingèd god's my plan.
Avoid all "magic" arts. Nor need you have recourse
    To secret potions from some newborn horse.   100
You can't make love thrive with Medea's witchy plants,
    Or Marsian charms mixed up with magic chants.
Both Circe and Medea lost their men. How could
    This be if witches' spells were any good?
Love philters, seasick-green? No profit's to be had.   105
    They harm the brain . . . and drive young women mad.
Abominations all. To get love, give love! *Live* it.
    No good looks or physique will ever give it.
I don't care if you're Nireus, belovèd of
    Homer, or Hylas, cursed with Naiads' love: 110
To hold your mistress and not wake up stunned to find
    You're left behind, your body needs a *mind*.
The body's brittle beauty breaks, small bit by bit,
    Each hour . . . until the years devour it.
Soon, violets die—and lilies, opening like a horn;   115
    The rose, when blown, bequeaths the world a thorn.

So, handsome boy: soon, white hairs will be coming in,
    And soon, the furrows that will line your skin.
So build a hardy soul to grace your body's form;
    As funeral coals die out, the soul's still warm.   120
Take care to learn the liberal arts; the girls you seek
    Admire Roman men who know their Greek.
Though plain, Ulysses spoke with sweet fluidity;
    For him, sea goddesses gave up the sea.
Calypso wept each time he tried to row away,   125
    Saying the sea was "wrong for oars today."
Over and over she would have Troy's fallen glory
    From him: in fresh new words, the same old story.
Sharing the shore, the lovely goddess stood and waited
    To hear king Rhesus' cruel fate narrated.   130
Ulysses, with a staff (by chance, he had a staff),
    Drew in the sand that story's bloody graph.
"Here's Troy," he says, tracing a sandy wall or ramp,
    "And Simois. Pretend this is my camp.
Here is the plain (he draws a plain) where Dolon bleeds,   135
    Dying while trying for Achilles' steeds.
There lie the tents of Rhesus, king of Thrace. That night,
    I rode his horses captured in our fight."
Then diagramming Rhesus, Troy, and so much more,
    He saw a wave come wash them from the shore.   140
Calypso said, "Those waves you think will carry you
    Away, will, as with these names, bury you."

So all of you, believe in beauty cautiously.
    Try for an inner beauty—*that's* the key.
To win her heart, a deft indulgence counts for more   145
    Than harshness, which can lead to civil war.

We hate the hawk because his warring will not sleep;
    We hate the wolf who hunts the bleating sheep.
But gentle swallows are no enemies of ours,
    And peaceful doves live in Chaonian towers.   150
Stay far away from biting words and bitter battle;
    Love thrives on honeyed tongues and sweet talk's prattle.
Let bickering wives chase husbands (and then versa-vice),
    Thinking they're "meant" to pay this marriage price.
(If wives bring *this* for dowry, bickering abounds.   155
    But always pipe your lover lovely sounds.)
To think *law* sanctions bedding her, well . . . that's a flaw;
    For you, it's love that takes the place of law.
Bring her sweet nothings—words that she'll delight to hear—
    So when you come to see her, she will cheer!   160
I've come to teach the poor, not those who have no need.
    You bauble-buyers: I'm not the bard to read.
Rich men, who when they please, can say, "My dear, take this"
    Are "skilled" enough to give *my* verse a miss.
Poor poet Naso loved once. When he had designs,   165
    He couldn't buy girls gifts; he fed them lines.
So let the pauper shun mean words, and love with care,
    Carrying burdens rich men wouldn't bear.
I think of how—irate—I mussed my mistress' hair:
    How many days did anger cost me there?   170
I *didn't* rip her dress. At least that was *my* sense
    Of it, but she said so . . . to my expense.
So if you're wise, avoid your teacher's gaffes at love
    And you won't do what he was guilty of.
Fight Parthians, then, but with a lover, keep the peace   175
    And gaily practice what makes love increase.

Now if she's not a willing girl who wants to lead
　　You on, persist, and she will soon concede.
Compliance bends the curving branch that otherwise
　　Would break; if you manhandle it, it dies.   180
Compliance helps us swim the seas, but if we fight
　　Their currents, we will fail despite our might.
The bull, by steps, yields to the plough. Numidian lions
　　And tigers soon grow tame by wise compliance.
Take Atalanta: *stubborn.* An Arcadian mule,   185
　　She fought a hero, but still lost that duel.
They say he often sat beneath some leafy scrim
　　And moaned about the way she treated him.
He'd lug around huge hunting nets—one of his chores—
　　And use steel blades to spear the savage boars.   190
He felt that wound the bow strung by Hylaeus dealt,
　　Though soon, another's bow was what he felt.
But I won't make you climb up Maenalus's slope
　　In armor, hauling nets against all hope.
No, there's no need to bare your breast to whizzing arrows;   195
　　My art's commands rest lighter than some Pharaoh's.
If she fights back, you yield; by yielding, you will win.
　　Just play the part for which you're pencilled in.
If she complains, complain, and bless the things she blesses;
　　Deny when she denies; yes when she yesses.   200
Laugh when she laughs; cry if she cries. Always take care
　　To let her face teach your face what to wear.
Suppose she's gaming, rolling ivory tesserae:
　　Roll yours awry, or give your roll the lie.
With large dice, should she lose, don't let her pay what's due,   205
　　But rig things so the "dog" pass falls to you.
At "Robbers," let your token-stone be taken by

Her glassy token; let your "soldier" die.
Carry her rib-taut parasol yourself, and be
    Her bodyguard through mobbed humanity.   210
Be quick to put her footstool where it should be put,
    And ease the slipper from her slender foot.
No matter if you're shivering, be sure to chafe
    Her hands inside your toga, warm and safe.
Don't think that it demeans (it does, but it *will* please),   215
    So hold her mirror up to what she sees.
That one who one day won the skies his back had borne
    (When Hera tired of all her monstrous scorn),
Once stayed among Ionian girls. His basket full,
    He acted maid-like, spinning un-worked wool.   220
If Hercules obeyed a mistress's command,
    Then why *you* won't is hard to understand.
If summoned to the Forum, come ahead of time—
    And don't leave early (that would be a crime).
She wants you somewhere? Stop! And run without delay;   225
    Don't let the madding crowd get in your way.
And should she want you with her when some banquet's done—
    An escort home—then be her slave . . . and run!
Love frowns on sloth, so if you're out of town and still
    She summons you, start walking with a will,   230
And don't let lethal heat in August make you slow,
    Or sluggish roads gone white with sudden snow.

Now, love is war by other means; the weak of heart
    Can't bear its banners. Timid men, depart!
Sweet Amor means the dark, the cold, long roads to tramp;   235
    It's hard, the labor where *he* pitches camp.
A thousand clouds will batter you; you'll think you've drowned,

Sleeping—and freezing—on the rocky ground.
Apollo herded King Admetus' kine, they say,
    And occupied a hut, hidden away.   240
So Phoebus suffered no more than you ought to bear;
    Cast off your pride if lasting love's your care.
Suppose the way's not clear, and reaching her's a chore.
    What *if* your Katie's keeper bars the door?
Just slip yourself headfirst down her compluvium!   245
    High windows, too, are good to come in from.
Then she'll rejoice to know you risked your neck for her,
    Proving that she's your Lady, you, her Sir.
Leander could have left his love to fret and stew,
    Yet swam the Hellespont to prove it true.   250

Don't be ashamed to cultivate her maids (from low
    To high); her slaves can help as well, you know.
Salute them all by name (it costs you nothing) and
    Ambitious as you are, shake each one's hand.
What if some slave should beg a gift? It won't cost much. 255
    A gift on Good Luck Day: that's a nice touch.
Give to the maids to mark that day when Gauls saw "wives"
    In slaves and paid the highest price—their lives.
Believe me: cultivate the low-born janitor
    And *know* the one who guards her bedroom door.   260
Mind you, I don't advise expensive gifts at all,
    But cunning trinkets shrewdly picked ... and small.
When wheat-fields teem and ponderous branches nod with fruit,
    Your boy should take your girl some; *that* should suit.
Tell her you grew them on your country place—"the farm."   265
    (Some Via Sacra pears will do no harm.)
Or send her grapes, or nuts that once, "in days of yore,"

Sweet "Amaryllis loved" . . . but loves no more.
In fact, a dove or thrush will testify you love her,
    And prove the fact that you're still thinking of her.   270
(It's foul giving to old folks so they'll change their will.
    I say those are givers we ought to kill!)

I *don't* say send her tender verses, though, since verse
    Wins precious little honor . . . more's the curse.
Oh, poems *do* get praised—when money does the talking   275
    And prizes go to rich barbarians squawking.
This really *is* the Age of Gold: the price is gold
    For honor and for love, both bought and sold.
Homer, if you came served by all the Muses, yet
    Were broke, then Homer, how far would you get?   280
Sure, *some* girls have good taste, but most have taste that's bad.
    Some have no taste at all, but wish they had.
Just praise them all, in any kind of verse, and "sell"
    Her on its quality by reading well.
That way, they'll all consider every piece a gem   285
    You've written as a present just for them.

Whatever useful thing you long had planned to do,
    Always be sure your lover asks you to.
Some slave, say, who has won your pledge to set him free,
    Should beg your mistress for his liberty.   290
He's due a whipping? Biting chains? Grant him a stay;
    She'll owe for what you'd scheduled anyway!
The profit's yours, but just be sure *she* gets the praise,
    Playing at Lady Bountiful for days.
But if you really want to keep your passion deathless,   295
    Convince her that her beauty leaves you breathless.

If she's in Tyrian, feed your dear your Tyrian line;
    If she's in Coan silk, Coan's *divine*.
In gold? Then she's "more precious than the finest gold."
    In wool? Then wool will have to be extolled.   300
If nothing but her slip is on, say you're aflame,
    Then ask her if she's cold (be shy and tame).
If she should part her hair, then praise that very part.
    Suggest her curling iron brands your heart!
Worship her voice and say she dances like a top;   305
    Beg her that neither charm should ever stop.
Tell her she makes love like a dream—and don't be coy!
    Nothing she does could "give [you] greater joy."
If she's Medusa in your arms—and you get bitten—
    Swear it's "a dove" with which your heart's been smitten.   310
But *never* let your face give anything away:
    Your thoughts are what your face should not betray.
True art is best concealed; revealed, it's sure to shame,
    And—rightly—rob you of your honest name.

Often, in autumn, season of most lovelinesses,   315
    Which fills all grapes that purple ripeness blesses,
When chilly mists oppress and sunshine melts the skin,
    The blood subsides; uncertain air comes in.
Let's hope she's well, but if she should take sickly, whether
    From heat or cold, suffering under the weather,   320
Then show your girl that you're devoted—make it clear—
    And as you sow, reap later, without fear.
Then don't let sickbed squeamishness come over you;
    No! Make your hands do all she wants you to.
Cry openly: she'll beg your kiss; you'll take your dear's.   325
    Perhaps with parched lips she will drink your tears.

Make many vows, and face-to-face. Come up with all
    The happy dreams your "memory" can recall.
Call in some crone to purify her boudoir's bed
    With eggs and sulphur . . . and with palsied tread.   330
All this will prove your love and please her wonderfully.
    (It's won more than one man a legacy!)
Still, don't grow unctuous with care; that might offend her;
    It's tactful service you're supposed to render.
And let her eat; don't ply her with some bitter juice.   335
    Leave *that* to rivals woefully obtuse.

The winds that helped you leave the shore will blow in vain
    When you go sailing on the bounding main.
Young love is errant, but it *needs* to get around;
    The time and practice make it strong and sound.   340
That bull you fear, you petted when it wasn't big;
    What now you sleep beneath was once a twig.
That little stream, in gaining waters as it goes,
    Grows stronger, till at last a river flows.
Make *her* grow used to you, accustomed to your face;   345
    Work at it till your presence falls in place.
Let her lend you her ear; become a constant sight,
    Showing your features to her day and night.
And when you're certain that she'll miss you—that she'll care
    About the fact that you're some other where—   350
Leave her alone. A fallow field soon shows its worth,
    And rain is best absorbed by arid earth.
Demophöon could barely fire Phyllis' heart—
    At home—till he decided to depart.
Wily Ulysses' absence teased Penelope;   355
    Laodamia, too, mourned grievously.

But keep your absence brief (love *can* grow cold in time),
　　Or "out of sight" and "out of mind" may rhyme!
With Helen's husband gone, she scorned to sleep alone,
　　Slipping into her guest's bed, not her own.   360
O Menelaus, what a fool! Your wife and *guest*?
　　A cretin could have guessed the sorry rest.
Insanity, handing a hunting hawk a dove,
　　Or trusting sheepfolds wolves are keepers of!
I don't blame Helen, nor is Paris much to blame: 365
　　He cheated, but *you* would have done the same.
In fact, you threw these two together, till by dint
　　Of . . . well, you see: compelled, they took your hint.
What else should she have done, considering her fear
　　Of half-filled beds, with charming Paris near?   370
So, why should Helen's amorous actions be resented?
　　She only seized the chance her lord presented.

However . . . when the roan-red boar, his fierce tusks flashing,
　　Savages rabid dogs, tossing and slashing,
Or lionesses offer un-weaned cubs the teat,   375
　　Or vipers feel the crush of careless feet,
They can't compare to women catching rivals slinking
　　Around; *then* faces flame with what they're thinking!
Decorum cast aside, she hunts for torch and sword—
　　A raging Maenad Bacchus' horns have gored.   380
The foreign Phasian took revenge on Jason, who
　　Had cheated on her, through the sons she slew.
Procne's another dire mother, on whose breast
　　You see, in blood, the swallow-sign impressed.
So solid love dissolves when cheating comes to light;   385
　　Such sins should give the cautious man a fright!

And yet my warning shouldn't mean you're stuck with one.
> Good god! A *bride* would let you have more fun.
Yes, play around, but quietly. And keep it hidden.
> Don't look for glory out of what's forbidden.   390
Too many gifts will give it all away. Fixed times
> Are also bad for cheating's little crimes.
And don't get caught because your love nest is well known,
> And all your girls have used that one alone.
When writing, smooth the wax of words your hand erases;   395
> Too many women read old letters' traces!
A wounded Venus rightly fights back, wounding you;
> She makes you feel the pain *she's* subject to.
While Agamemnon kept one wife, that wife he kept
> Was chaste, *then* changed the man with whom she slept.   400
(She'd heard that Chryses, filleted and bearing laurel,
> Had lost his daughter in the chieftains' quarrel.
She'd heard, O captive Briseis, how you'd been wronged,
> And how delays meant war would be prolonged—
But only *heard*. Cassandra stood before her *eyes*;   405
> The "victor" was the prize of his own prize).
That's when she took Aegisthus to her heart . . . and bed,
> And cut two-timing Agamemnon dead.

If what you've well concealed should nonetheless be known, it
> Is best denying what's revealed: disown it.   410
And afterward, not too much yielding flattery,
> Which makes you look as guilty as can be.
But spare no effort. One thing only brings sure peace:
> Sex makes her wrath at sexual rivals cease.
Some teach that you should take up savory, but I   415
> Say no; it's noxious poison and you'll die.

Some say use nettle seed, with pepper pounded fine,
    Or chamomile ground up in agèd wine.
But she high Eryx keeps upon his shady hills
    Won't yield her grace to simples, herbs, and pills.   420
Eat *onions* sent from Megara to help you harden,
    And rocket, lewd, and fresh out of the garden.
Hymettian honey works, and eating eggs as well;
    Try needled-pine nuts; they should make you swell.

But learnèd Erato, why magic arts and drugs?   425
    Now watch the inner post my chariot hugs!
And you I was just counseling to hide your sin,
    I counsel changing course: confess! Give in!
Don't blame my "flighty" ways, though. Ships that ply the seas
    Carry their crews by more than just one breeze,   430
Flying before the North Wind now, and next the South,
    Sails full into the West or East Wind's mouth.
Consider how the chariot driver slacks the reins
    Of horses that his sure art then restrains.
Well, some girls you indulge will show no gratitude: 435
    Unrivaled love soon means a languorous mood.
Proud spirits often bask in their success and fail
    To deal with what good fortune can entail.
A fire dying bit by bit, its force all gone,
    Makes ashes hide the sparks they're lying on.   440
Add sulphur, though, to fire, and soon again it burns;
    Yes, light that blazed before, once more returns.
Well that's what sluggish hearts do when they're free of care;
    A few sharp pricks must make their passion flare.
So make her doubt you; fire up her tepid feelings.   445
    She'll blanch at word of all your double-dealings.

Oh, four times happy—happier than man can say—
    Is he a love-wronged woman fears may stray!
(When nasty rumors reach that girl's unwilling ears,
    She's pale and speechless, fainting from her fears).   450
Let it be me whose hair that woman tries to shred;
    Let it be me whose cheeks her nails rip red.
I want her seeing me through eyes gone grim from crying,
    And saying that without me, she is dying.

How long this moaning over wrongs? Shorter, not longer,   455
    So slow delay can't make her rage grow stronger.
Before that comes, her soft white neck should be the place
    Your arms begin their "dry-your-tears" embrace.
Kiss her, and as she cries, make love; you'll soon have peace.
    This is the one way anger finds release.   460
When she has raged her fill, and seems your foe for sure,
    The truce of sex will make true peace endure.
The goddess Concord lives where weapons are forsworn;
    There—trust me—reconciling Grace is born,
And doves who only now were fighting, turn to wooing,   465
    And bill-to-beak, speak love words with their cooing.

All jumbled in a mass, before true order came,
    The stars and earth and seas looked all the same.
Then Earth received the sky, and waters ringed the land,
    Leaving blank chaos to its own remand.   470
Birds filled the air and beasts the places rich in trees;
    You fish lay hidden, lurking in the seas.
Then mankind wandered in the lonely fields, mere brutes
    With feral bodies, snuffling up raw roots
In forests, sleeping on what leaf-beds they could find.   475

For ages, men did not know their own kind.
It's said that pleasures softened up that savage race.
   A man and woman stopping in one place
Learned what to do to please themselves; they were self-taught
   In love-work done without a second thought.   480
Each bird has one whom he will love; at sea, each fish
   Will find a mate to gratify her wish.
The hind goes with her buck; snakes wind with other snakes.
   The bitch's hound—see what a bond he makes!
Rams leap on ewes, and bulls make happy heifers dote.   485
   The filthy billy humps his snub-nosed goat.
Mares crash through streams and wastelands, frenzied by the forces
   That drive them on to stallions (such are horses).
To sum up: bring strong medicines for women's rage;
   Such stringent formulas alone assuage.   490
These "medicines" surpass Machaon's juices; these,
   When you have wronged your woman, will appease.

Now while I sing this way, who but Apollo comes,
   Bearing the golden lyre that he strums.
With laurel in his hands and laurel in his hair,   495
   He speaks—the poet-god beyond compare:
"Preceptor of Lascivious Love: my temple's known
   Throughout the world. Your pupils should be shown
Its stone-carved admonition; order them to go
   And learn it is themselves that they must know.   500
For only those who wisely know themselves love well
   And find that in their projects they excel.
So if you see you're handsome, let those features shine,
   Or fair-skinned shoulders show when you recline.
Your tones are dulcet? Break the ice and speak your part.   505

A singer? Sing! A drinker? Ply your art!
But don't let stentors start up in the midst of talk,
　　Or crazy poets pose and prate and squawk."
So said great Phoebus—Phoebus, who's to be obeyed.
　　In that god's sacred mouth, the truth is made.   510

So, once again: whoever reads my *Art* will win
　　At love, as whom he wisely wants gives in.
But fields don't always pay back seeds with bumper crops,
　　Nor breezes rescue ships when good luck stops.
No, lovers garner little help, but lots of hurt,   515
　　Bracing for all those things that may subvert.
(As grazing hares on Athos, or as Hybla's bees;
　　Like olives thick on Pallas' gray-green trees,
Or conchs that dot the shore: these are love's grieving hearts,
　　The targets of a thousand poison darts.)   520
Her maid will say, "She's out," when you can plainly see
　　She's in. All right, she's "out." What's perjury?
On Assignation Night, you find her door's been barred.
　　Endure! Sit on that ground so vile and hard.
Maybe some maid, mendacious, with a haughty face,   525
　　Says, "Who's this beggar here? He's a disgrace!"
That's when to coax cruel girl and gate. Wheedle! Implore!
　　And hang your crown of roses on her door.
When she's unwilling, leave; when she'll receive you, go.
　　The well-bred man who nags has sunk too low.   530
Don't let her have the chance to say, "I can't get *rid*
　　Of him!" (She might regret it if she did.)
Till then, it's not so bad if she decides to beat—
　　Or lash—you; go ahead and kiss her feet.

Why pause for trivia when greater themes still call? 535
    I'll sing them if you'll listen, one and all.
(For art is hard, and what's not hard is not worthwhile;
    My art demands hard labor, test, and trial.)
Suffer a rival gladly, for you'll win out still,
    A victor on the Capitol—Jove's hill. 540
Dodonian oaks—not I—prophetically have spoken.
    This is the one great law that can't be broken:
She writes your rival? Let her. If she calls, obey.
    To come *or* go, be sure she has her way.
Well, even husbands let their lawful wives get by 545
    With this (soft sleep will shut a winking eye).
And yes, I know: I don't do as I say, it's true;
    My preaching's all unpracticed. What to do?
Just stand there as these flirting men display their sleaze?
    Before *that*, . . . Rage, come drive me where you please. 550
(My rival kissed her once; I made it plain to see
    My rage—which matched my love's barbarity.)
This vice has cost me more than once. A wiser man
    Lets others come as often as he can.
But just not knowing's best! Let women hide affairs; 555
    You want her blushes showing she still cares.
Young lovers, spare your energy and let girls cheat,
    Feeding you a long line of deft deceit.
Detection only makes things worse: the couple caught
    Keeps cheating, and your effort's all for naught. 560
The tale's told 'round the world of Mars and Venus brought
    Down by the nets that Mulciber had wrought.
Our father, Mars, half-mad for Venus, soon was sorry
    To see himself—once Captain—now Love's quarry.
It's true! Tender Venus cast no coy rustic's glances 565

At Mars, but more-than-welcomed his advances.
    They say she often laughed at Vulcan's crippled foot,
    And hands art-tempered in the fire and soot.
She'd imitate that limp for Mars, and it was charming,
    How grace and beauty mixed. That they were harming   570
Marriage, they knew, of course, and knew they were to blame;
    At first, they sinned, and sinning, felt some shame.
But then the tell-tale Sun (and who can fool the Sun?)
    Told Vulcan just what Mars's lust had done.
A bad example you were setting, Sun! Blackmail   575
    Venus and she'll "deliver" without fail.
So Vulcan sets his bed-trap, netting carefully—
    With handicraft so fine, no eye can see—
Then makes "for Lemnos." Soon, as planned, love's interlude—
    And implication, as they lie there nude.   580
Olympus' smithy calls the gods: the pair appears
    So ludicrous that Venus fights back tears.
They cannot hide their faces, Heaven's sorry lovers,
    Or reach the private parts their sin uncovers.
Some laughing someone says, "Brave Mars, if they should be   585
    Too much for you, transfer your chains to me!"
Since Neptune asks, the smith frees them from their embrace—
    Barely. To Paphos, Venus. Mars? To Thrace.
But Vulcan, look what you have done: they hid, before,
    What they do freely now! Shame's out the door.   590
Some say you see how foolish you have been, that this was ill-
    Done, and now you repent your art and skill.
So reader, heed my warning: clearly, Venus' case
    Means *don't* confront your mistress's disgrace.
Prepare no traps for rivals. Intercept no note   595
    Suspicion makes you think that either wrote.

Let men the marriage rites will turn to husbands waste
    Time trapping rivals they think should be chased.
Again, I swear: the law allows all games I play,
    So primly-skirted matrons, stay away!   600

Who'd dare profane the mysteries of Ceres or
    Expose great Samothrace's holy lore?
Holding your tongue's a modest virtue; giving in
    To whispering sacred rites, a heinous sin.
(That Tantalus should reach in vain to pluck a pear   605
    Is right. He thirsts, though water's everywhere.)
Venus commands her rites should not be spoken of;
    I warn you talkers: stay away from Love.
For even if no strong-box hides her mysteries,
    And beaten gongs warn off no *hes* and *shes*,   610
And love is practiced in our midst most commonly,
    Still, in our midst, she wants us not to see.
Venus herself, should she stand naked, half bends over,
    Her left hand placed to lend her *mons* some cover.
Mere beasts will mate in public, true—most anyplace.   615
    But seeing them, a girl averts her face.
The bedroom door should hide our furtive acts, while sheet
    And blanket keep our private parts discreet.
And if not shadows, then we seek, if not quite night,
    At least less open light, or the half-light.   620
Back when the sun and rain both knew no tiles stood proof
    Against them; when the oak gave food and roof,
We loved inside a cave or underneath that oak,
    Which shows what shame once meant to simple folk.
But now! Our nighttime deeds lead man to boast and swagger,   625
    And at a fearful cost, become a bragger.

Of course, they have to try for every girl, so they
    Can say, "With that one, too, I've had my way."
(Embarrassing, should one run short of girls to finger.)
    And as you point, you're each girl's vile mudslinger?   630
But these are trifles. Men invent things they'd deny
    If true, then claim a thousand trysts (they lie—
And foul the names of bodies that they've never touched;
    The body stays intact; the name gets smutched).
Yes, odious custodian: go close her door—   635
    A hundred bolts you've never thrown before!
Whose name is safe from what some vile defiler does
    Who's out retailing that which never was?
Even my true loves I keep dark. Believe you me,
    They're wrapped deep in a solid secrecy.   640

Don't rush to point her faults out. Spare her; let them be
    Faults that most have pretended not to see.
Andromeda's complexion didn't mean a thing
    To Perseus, whose heels each wore a wing.
Andromache was way too big in people's eyes,   645
    But Hector thought his wife the perfect size.
What you've borne ill, bear well. Long love is tolerant toward
    So many faults new lovers once abhorred.
While fresh green grafts grow slowly in the bark of trees,
    The tender slips succumb to any breeze.   650
But growing hardy over time, they stand the gale.
    New fruit appears from stock that once was frail.
Time clears all flesh of what the world accounts a blot,
    Till what was once a body's fault is not.
Young noses cannot bear to smell a tanning hide;   655
    With time, they breathe what they could not abide.

Names soften things. The girl whose blood is blacker than
    Illyrian tar can wear "a dusky tan."
Gray-haired? "Minerva." "Venus" if just one straight eye.
    Say "slender" when her diet means she'll die.   660
A runt's "petite"; a fat girl's "stately" figure "awes."
    Near-virtues hide a multitude of flaws.

Who was Consul at her birth? Her age? *Don't ask.*
    That sort of question is the Censor's task.
(Especially if her salad days are past, her cares   665
    Come down to those of searching out gray hairs.)
Young men, that age is best—or even later on.
    That field will bear; it's ripe for being sown.   668
What's more, these older women know just what to do.
    Experience has made them artful, too!   676
They compensate for age with elegance, while knowing
    The way to keep time's ruthless years from showing.
Their thousand modes of love? Whatever you require:
    No book could show more ways to quench desire.   680
To satisfy their wants, they don't need prompts or spurs;
    What pleases you should be both yours and hers.
I hate it when two lovers don't conclude wrung out.
    (That's why I don't indulge in boys, no doubt.)
I hate the girl whom Duty calls to do her sinning;   685
    Bone-dry, she lies there . . . thinking of her spinning.
When pleasure's grudging, then it's pleasure that can't please;
    "Dutiful" girls will only make me freeze.
I want her words—as wild as woman's words can get;
    I want to hear "Yes! Yes!" and yet "Not yet!"   690
I want to see her gray eyes rolling back so much,
    Till languishing, she cannot bear my touch.

Youth doesn't know these joys, which Nature still withholds
    From all but seasoned thirty-five-year-olds.
Let hasty types drink callow wine; some vintage jar   695
    From olden days I much prefer by far.
You'll find no sun-shade under sycamores half-grown,
    And bare feet bleed from meadow grass just sown.
Faced with Hermione, you'd take her mother? Choose a
    Helen, or pick a Gaea, not Medusa?   700
Well, those who want their lovers skilled should apprehend
    That patience wins love's prizes in the end.

Look: lovers on a bed that seems almost aware.
    But doors close now; our Muse must halt right there.
Without my Muse, this pair will know just what to say,   705
    And four hands where to go, in every way.
Their fingers will find what to do deep in those parts
    That Amor touches with his secret darts.
Andromache and mighty Hector did this, too.
    (Warfare was not the only art he knew.)   710
The great Achilles, too, with his Briseis, weighing
    Down the soft bed when he was done with slaying.
Briseis, you allowed his touch—those hands dyed deep
    In Phrygian blood. Were you so lewd, so cheap
Beneath Achilles, that you found that prospect thrilling—   715
    Your flesh explored by someone fresh from killing?
Trust me: the joy of sex should not be rushed, but bit-
    By-bit brought on by slowly balking it.
Finding that place where she will love to feel your touch,
    Don't let some shyness slow you down *too* much.   720
Then watch her eyes go glittering, their light aquiver
    The way the sun will sparkle off a river.

Suiting her words to all your playful deeds, she'll sweetly
　　Sigh, moan, and murmur, pleasing you completely.
Don't crowd on sail to win this "race"—a big mistake—　　725
　　Or let her horses dust you in their wake.
Instead, the goal should be dead heat—the fullest measure
　　When both lie spent in their pursuit of pleasure.
Make this your practice: plough as if you had all day
　　When fear is not a factor in your play.　　730
But when delay's not safe, then lean into your oars as
　　Much as you can and prick your racing horses!
While years allow, keep at this work—while you're still strong;　　669*
　　Soon, bent old age will come limping along.
So split the sea with oar, or plough the soil with share,
　　Or try your bloody hand at war somewhere.
Bring to young women all your strength and heart and hands;
　　Your diligence is what such "war" demands.　　674*

My work is done. So grateful men, bestow the palm
　　And wreathe my hair with fragrant myrtle balm.
Danaan Podalirius could heal with skill.　　735
　　Achilles was a man no man could kill.
Nestor in counsel; Ajax, arms; Calchas as seer;
　　Automedon with whip: I am their peer
As lover! Honor me as bard and sing your praise
　　Worldwide, until the end of all our days.　　740
I've armed you just as Mulciber armed Thetis' son,
　　And with this gift you'll win the way *he* won.
Who wins his Amazon by my instruction, though,
　　Should write that "Naso taught me all I know."

But look! Waiting for my advice, you girls shall be　　745
　　My poem's next concern. Turn to Book Three.

BOOK III

I've armed you Greeks against the Amazons, and mean
    To do the same for them and for their queen.
Go battle equally! It's in Dione's hands
    And in her son's, who flies through far-flung lands.
Defenseless women fighting men? It's not the same,   5
    And victory would only bring men shame.
Now some might ask, "Why give more venom to a snake,
    Or lambs to she-wolves with a thirst to slake?"
Well, don't blame everyone for bad seed some have sown;
    Instead, judge each young woman on her own.   10
True, Helen left poor Menelaus badly used,
    And yes, her sister stood justly accused.
It's true as well Eriphyle once had her mate
    Steed-drawn, to meet—alive—his Stygian fate.
But chaste Penelope stood by her wily lord,   15
    Who ten long years had wandered, ten years warred.
Think of Protesilaus' wife, of whom it's said
    She rushed to join her spouse but lately dead.
And then, Alcestis saved Admetus' forfeit life
    By dying for him, like a perfect wife.   20
"O husband, let our ashes mix," Evadne cried,
    Then leapt upon the funeral pyre and died.
Virtue herself's a woman, both by dress and name;
    Plainly, she pleases those who seem the same.
Such minds are not required by the art I draft;   25

Less noble sails become its modest craft.
As I instruct the world in wanton love alone,
    How men should love them, women will be shown.
And when do women shake their brands or brandish bows?
    One seldom sees these used against male foes.   30
No, men deceive the most; with women, it is rare
    (Committing fraud). Research it if you dare!
When Jason sent away his pregnant mate, he lied,
    Then wrapped his arms around another bride.
Or Theseus: Ariadne, left some God-knows-where,   35
    Might have been bait for gulls. But did *you* care?
To learn how Nine Ways got its name, one stops and hears
    "For Phyllis, forests shed their leaves like tears."
Dido, the title "Pious" was your love's reward;
    He left you—hinting death—his naked sword.   40
Ladies: why did you fail? To make love last forever
    Requires skill; it's art that makes you clever!
And that's where I'd have left things, but . . . Venus appears
    And tells me, "Teach them, the defenseless dears."
She asked me, "Why have you betrayed my women, then,   45
    Turning them over to armed mobs of men
Books One and Two instructed men in all my arts;
    Now girls must learn the skills your verse imparts.
That bard who spewed abuse of wifely Helen soon
    Struck up a better lyre and changed his tune.   50
If I know you (who'd never scorn such cultured pearls),
    You'll spend your lifetime cultivating girls."
Done, Venus took a myrtle leaf and berries from
    The garland round her hair and gave me some.
Accepting them, I sensed their numen: all the air   55
    Shone purely, and my heart was free of care.

While Venus moves me still, here learn your skills, girls—you
    Whom custom, law, and right permit this to.
For now's the time to think of all those years to come,
    Before old age and waste have left you numb.   60
While you still can, and salad days are not yet gone,
    Play! Nothing stops the years from flowing on.
It can't return, that wave that breaks up on the shore,
    Just as an hour passed will come no more.
Seize Time; his swift foot can't be held. But here's the worst: 65
    What follows never equals what came first.
These withered stalks I see were violets once, this thorn
    A braided chaplet that my brows have worn.
There'll come a day when you who now shut out your lovers
    Will lie like frozen hags beneath night's covers.   70
Outside your door at night? No battles going on.
    (Nor roses scattered at that door at dawn.)
It's sad how soon flesh furrows! Then, it comes undone,
    And faces fade that once shone like the sun.
White hairs you'll swear you've had since you were just a girl   75
    Will suddenly appear in every curl.
Now, serpents slough old age each time they shed their skin;
    Stags drop their racks to make new life begin.
Our charms depart all on their own, so pluck the bloom.
    For if you don't, it meets a wasted doom.   80
And this: with every child you bear, youth's fate is sealed.
    (A constant harvest ages any field.)
On Latmos, Luna loves Endymion with pride.
    Is Cephalus some shame that Dawn must hide?
Though Venus had Adonis (whom she'll always mourn),   85
    How were Aeneas and Harmonia born?
O mortal girls, let all your models be divine:

When amorous men come asking, don't decline.
Even deceived, what have you lost? You have it still,
    After a thousand men have worked their will.   90
Flint thins from constant use, and iron rusts from wear,
    But do not fear: *that* part will still be there.
Who'd care if you "stole" torchlight? Isn't fire free?
    Who'd guard the waters of the boundless sea?
So when a woman tells a man, "It's best we don't,"   95
    Will she lose water that he's drawn? She won't.
I don't say "sell yourself," but only "have no fear
    Of phantom loss." No gift is "lost," my dear.
Though soon to launch out through the force of fiercer gales,
    While I'm in port, let zephyrs fill my sails.   100

Let's start with cultivation: body, crops, or soil,
    Good vines and wheat require careful toil.
Beauty's a god-like gift of which few girls can boast
    Because it's truly been denied to most.
Care forms the face; neglect your face, there's no survival—   105
    Not even if it once was Venus' rival.
True, girls of old gave bodies little care, but then,
    They seldom dealt with cultivated men!
Andromache was dressed in coarse wool tunics, true,
    But what was rugged Hector's wife to do?   110
No doubt the wife of Ajax went in silk to greet
    A husband dressed in seven plies of meat!
Once, Rome was rough and simple; now it's made of gold,
    With all the wealth the conquered world can hold.
Look at our Capitol; think what it used to be.   115
    Two Joves lived there, all changèd utterly.
The Senate, which in Tatius' time was made of clay

And wattles, is far nobler in *our* day.
That lofty hill where Phoebus and our leaders shine—
    Once cattle pasture—is the Palatine.   120
Let others love the past; born yesterday, I'm *glad!*
    These times are best—the best I've ever had.
But not because men mine the earth for golden ores,
    And shells come gathered from a thousand shores,
Or cliffs shrink, marble fossicked out, year after year,   125
    While blue bay waters flee the rich man's pier.
But for our splendid *cultivation*, and the way
    Those "good old" manners are not ours today.

And yet, take precious pearls: don't load your ears with these
    The swarthy Indian gathers from green seas.   130
Don't gad about with gold sewn in your clothes; such stitches,
    Meant to attract, repel with gaudy riches.
It's *elegance* we like, so coif yourself with care;
    The merest touch can make for lovely hair.
(There's more than just one style. What suits each girl the best,   135
    Her mirror knows. That's how it should be dressed.)
A long face needs a part severe and plain—the style
    Laodamia wore it in . . . awhile.
A loose-knit knot on top best suits round faces, though;
    That way, the lady's lovely ears can show.   140
One woman, shoulder-tressed, looks like the lyre's Lord,
    Apollo, as he strums some dulcet chord.
Another ties it back like girt Diana when
    She hunts the startled creatures through the glen.
One looks her best with flowing locks that lie there loose;   145
    Another pulls them tighter than a noose.
It pleases some to wear Cyllenian tortoise shells,

While others wear their hair in flowing swells.
But this is counting acorns in the branch-thick trees,
    Or all the alpine beasts, or Hybla's bees. 150
I'll never number all these fashions. What a chore!
    The next day only brings a hundred more.
Even when hair's "neglected," oh, since "days ago,"
    It can look good (just now, she combed it, though).
"I love Iole," said Alcides at first glance, 155
    Inside the captured town. Art mimics chance.
(Deserted Ariadne, too, at Bacchus' side
    Caught up: "Euoë!" all the Satyrs cried.)
Ladies, how Nature loves your charms, the faults of which
    Can be repaired in ways that are so rich! 160
Men lose their hairs as Time declares them at an end:
    The North Wind shakes the leaves; the leaves descend.
But a woman can dye her gray with German dyes;
    Art improves shades that Nature's will supplies.
A woman strolls the town in thick wigs bought with gold, 165
    Then buys new hair to complement the old.
And having bought, she doesn't blush! Right there she buys,
    Before Alcides' and the Muses' eyes.

What should I say of clothes? No flounces, please—not I—
    Or wool blushing purple with Tyrian dye. 170
Of many cheaper hues to wear, there's just no lack;
    It's mad to bear your fortune on your back!
Example: cloudless blue—sky-blue—the shade you see
    When tepid Auster keeps the air rain-free.
Or look: the gold the ram wore carrying away 175
    Ino's Phrixus and Helle—so they say.
"Sea-green" we call this color from the green-gray sea;

That nymphs would dress in it makes sense to me!
Here's one like crocus; dewy Dawn, in saffron cloak,
    Leads Lucifer and Lightborn to their yoke.   180
And Paphian myrtles? Purple amethysts? The white
    Of roses? Or, gray Thracian cranes in flight?
Yes, Amaryllis, chestnuts . . . and your almonds, too.
    "Cerina" gives the fleece a "waxy" hue.
It's like when vines grow warm: those blooms the new earth shows   185
    Grow loose from winter, and slow winter goes.
Count *those*! For that's how many dyes the wool will drink.
    Take care; not every shade is what you think:
Dark gray for pale skin; fair Briseis, snatched away,
    Wore what became her best—dark charcoal gray.   190
White's best for darker tones; Cepheis pleased in white,
    Which caused the isle of Seriphos's plight.

I almost warned, "No goat smell in your armpits, please,
    And bristling leg hairs? Shave your shins of these!"
But you aren't women from the Caucasus, or those   195
    Who drink from where the Mysian Caicus flows.
"Don't let your teeth turn brown from laziness; each day,
    Wash out your mouth": *that's* what I need to say?
You know already how to whiten skin with clay,
    And blush by art what wasn't made that way.   200
By art, you fill in eyebrows Nature drew too thin,
    And patch your cheeks with little scraps of skin.
You're not ashamed to paint your eyes with ashes or
    With saffron from the sparkling Cydnus' shore.
I wrote of beauty treatments for the face and hair—   205
    A little book, but one that took great care.
Learn there what you should do lest beauty fall apart;

It is no idle, useless thing, my art.
Art glories in its artificial face. No lover
    Should see your paint box; keep it undercover.   210
Who wouldn't be repulsed when stuff smeared on your face
    Melts down your chest, running its oily race?
These ointments stink; yes, even if they come from Greece,
    They're extracts processed from some filthy fleece.
Deer-marrow cream should not be put on openly,   215
    And *never* brush your teeth where *he* can see.
What makes you fair may not be pretty in the viewing;
    Things fair when *done* are vile when in the *doing*.
Statues that Myron signed to mark them as his own
    Were once no more than ponderous blocks of stone.   220
To make a ring means first you have to crush gold ore.
    Those clothes you wear were dirty wool before.
This famous cameo's form was once a rough-hewn rock's:
    Nude Venus wringing water from her locks.
Just so, we'll think you're "sleeping"—like that rock—while you   225
    Prepare the final touches for our view.
Why let me see what gives your face that "special" glow?
    Just close the door! It's far too soon to know.
Most things are never known by men, and that's just right:
    Most things offend . . . if not kept out of sight.   230
Those lavish golden playhouse figures look quite good;
    Get close, and you'd despise their gilded wood.
When gilding's just half-done, folks can't get near it yet.
    (Don't summon men until your beauty's set.)
Except . . . to comb your hair in public is all right—   235
    Locks draped across your back: a lovely sight!
But don't be fidgeting when you're upset; you'll play
    With your coiffure till it's in disarray.

And leave your maid alone! To scratch her face or stick
    Her arm with pins—that makes me simply sick.   240
She'll curse your head each time you touch her; then she cries,
    Bleeding on tresses you've made her despise.
Bad hair? Well, post a door guard; that should work just fine.
    Or have it done at Bona Dea's shrine.
I paid a call once, unannounced, on someone who   245
    Panicked, and put her hair on wrong-way-to—
A fate fit for my enemies alone: disgrace
    And shame for women of the Parthian race.
Polled cattle are as ugly as a grassless prairie,
    A leafless bush, or head no longer hairy.   250

Clearly, I teach no Leda and no Semele;
    Nor Europa, "bull"-borne across the sea.
Nor Helen, whom her husband—no fool—wanted back,
    But whom the crafty Paris kept . . . alack.
No, mostly average women read me—pretty, plain,   255
    And ugly—mostly ugly, in the main.
The beautiful by birth don't need the arts I preach;
    They *have* a dowry that no art can teach.
For when the sea's serene, the captain scants command.
    But when it storms, he calls for every hand.   260
Rare is the faultless face, so try to compensate
    For that . . . *and* body-faults; improve your fate!
If short, sit down—if standing makes men think you've sat
    (Reclining stretched out ought to cover that.
And even then, to baffle men with measuring eyes,   265
    Cover your feet; no one will guess your size.)
A skinny girl should wear the fullest-figured clothes;
    Be sure the gown, loose from her shoulders, flows.

Red stripes on pale girls hide a multitude of sins,
    While Pharian linen best sets off dark skins.   270
Bad feet are something dazzling, snow-white boots can hide.
    Thin shins should keep their laced-up leggings tied.
High collar bones need shoulder pads for leveling.
    To boost flat chests, enhancers are the thing.
No matter what you say, avoid hand gestures, please,   275
    If swollen fingers' nails flaunt some disease.
Eat first if fasting tends to make mouth odor reek,
    And stand back from your lover when you speak.
Don't laugh if you've a buck, or black, or crooked tooth;
    You'll pay an awful price, and that's the truth.   280

These days, The Laugh is part of female education!
    But even here there should be moderation.
No wide-mouth grinning, please, and keep those dimples small.
    The lips should barely show the teeth at all.
Ladies, don't herniate yourselves from non-stop laughter;   285
    Feminine trilling is the sound we're after.
One girl deforms her face with uproar's ugly drenching;
    Another weeps as if some grief were wrenching.
Then take guffawing laughs so raucous in their cawing
    You'd think a millstone ass were caught hee-hawing.   290
Where *doesn't* art come in? Crying to charm a man,
    Girls weep at will, whatever way they can.
They even cheat our Latin of its proper sound,
    Tongues lisping words their lips can't get around.
Slight defects charm, so girls talk poorly—or they try,   295
    Each speaking till her speaking powers die.
Spend time on all these things, for they can profit you:
    Carry yourself the way fine women do;

Even your step can show a certain charm. It both
    Attracts men and makes many of them loath.   300
One woman sways her hips, robes welcoming the breeze,
    And proudly points her toes just where they please.
Another steps out like a sunburnt farmer's bride,
    An Umbrian in her huge, clod-hopping stride.
But moderation in all things; I have no doubt   305
    It's just as bad to mince as stomp about.
And yet . . . it pleases me when pale-white women wear
    Their upper arms and lower shoulders bare.
Wherever lovely shoulders lie exposed like this
    I see the very skin I've got to kiss.   310

Now, at their will, the Sirens, monsters of the sea,
    Could stop a ship, they sang so beautifully.
(Ulysses heard—and nearly melted, drawing near;
    His sailors plugged their ears and could not hear.)
Seductive song! Girls: learn it and you'll gain allure,   315
    Getting the men your faces can't procure.
Sing songs you've heard in marble theatres, or play
    The latest tunes in the Egyptian way.
I wouldn't think you polished if you didn't know
    The proper hands where pick and lyre go.   320
Rhodopian Orpheus made rocks and wild beasts stir;
    His lyre tamed Tartarus' three-headed cur.
A just avenger who made Dirce soon atone,
    Amphion strummed to build Thebes' walls of stone.
Though dumb, a dolphin loved to hear Arion play   325
    And sing—a well-known story to this day.
Girls, learn to strum (both hands!) the nablus, heaven-sent,
    And fit for more-than-genial merriment.

Philitas and Callimachus should fill your head,
    And winey old Anacreon be read.   330
Read Sappho's Muse (lascivious as she can be),
    And him whose slaves pull off such trickery.
Be sure you can recite Propertius's verse,
    Tibullus's, or Gallus's; rehearse!
Know Varro and his golden fleece that caused your twin,   335
    Phrixus, such grief—the sea where she fell in.
And know Aeneas, Latium's founder, much revered;
    No greater work in Latin has appeared.
Perhaps they'll speak *my* name with these in the same breath,
    And Lethe will not mean my verse's death.   340
Perhaps they'll say, "His *Ars* makes Naso master of
    Both sexes' education touching love.
Or from the three books called *Amores*, make a choice
    Of something you can read with dulcet voice.
Or maybe sing some *Letter* that you're perfect in   345
    (With Ovid, letter-poems first begin)."
Oh, grant it, Phoebus! Grant it, Muses, poets dead
    And gone, and Bacchus of the hornèd head!

And who would doubt I think that girls should learn to dance?
    Set down your wine and sway with elegance!   350
We love the dancer's art we see on stage, in plays,
    For all the graceful charm that she displays.
Now, dice and such (I blush to add that you should know
    Mere knucklebones—and how to call and throw).
Girls: sometimes, roll a three and sometimes, plot whose side   355
    Your guile should take and whose should be defied.
Play cautiously at "Bandits"; use your brains if you
    Should lose one piece to an attack by two,

And find your champion battling on the field alone
>(For enemies return then; that's well known).   360
At "Marbles in the Net," move just the target ball,
>And with some luck, you *may* remove them all.
There is a game board ruled by just as many lines
>As the fleet year's black zodiac has signs.
Another game's small board requires, in a row,   365
>Three stones lined up to win (that's how you'll know).
Invent a thousand games not to be ignorant of;
>Games-playing: it's the entree to new love!
However . . . clever use of your next turn is *not*
>What counts. It's how to keep from getting hot!   370
That's when we grow oblivious, our true souls bared—
>When reckless passion leaves us unprepared
To hide the rage and greed that so deform the face.
>Our brawls and sorrows rob us of our grace,
As accusations fly and awful cries resound.   375
>We call on angry gods . . . and they are found.
The bankrupt wails, and begs a clean, new slate;
>That's when you see the tear ducts in full spate.
Jove keep you from such vile reproaches if you plan
>Ever to win yourself a clever man.   380

Soft Nature's given girls such slight frivolities,
>But men can sport with so much more than these.
They have their javelins, their balls, their hoops of steel,
>Their arms; they train their steeds to race and wheel.
She shuns the Campus and the Maid—they're made for him.   385
>Calm Tiber is a stream she will not swim.
But walking Pompey's Porch for shade—well, that's all right
>When Virgo's flaming steeds have reached their height.

Visit the laureled Phoebus' Palace if you're free.
    (He sank the ships of Egypt in the sea.)   390
Visit Octavia's and Livia's arcades,
    And his who won such naval accolades.
Visit the smoky shrines to Egypt's cow. Be sure
    You're seen at plays to show off your allure.
The Circus and arena, no one should forget—   395
    Where chariots race and blood-warm sands run wet.
What's hidden can't be known; the unknown cannot please;
    No prizes go to beauty no one sees.
Sing like those men who rivaled Phoebus in their fame!
    A lyre never heard wins no acclaim.   400
Consider Venus: had Apelles never brought her
    To "life," she'd still be waiting . . . underwater.
The sacred poets want no more than endless fame
    And glory; that's their labor's highest aim.
Once, poets were the chiefest care of god and king,   405
    And choruses won prizes when they'd sing.
Once, they were sanctified, their names all venerated,
    And often, hard-earned wealth was generated.
Ennius earned it, born in Italy's harsh toe;
    He's buried now beside great Scipio.   410
Now ivy is disgraced, and burning midnight oil
    For learnèd Muses mocked as idle toil.
But bards—like Homer—glory in the quest for fame;
    His *Iliad* un-penned, who'd know his name?
Or who'd have known of Danaë, locked in her tower   415
    And turning to a crone, hour by hour?
Beautiful girls, the public crowd can be of use,
    So get outside and walk a bit footloose.
To prey on just one lamb, wolves watch a dozen herds;

Jove's eagle plummets on whole flocks of birds.   420
That's how a beauty ought to let the public view her;
    She may find one who'll be attracted to her.
Earnest to please, she'll walk about in public places,
    Intent on making pretty, private faces.
Chance rules all things, so always keep your fishhook dangling;   425
    The poorest pools may mean the richest angling.
Dogs often chase a deer—all over dale and hill—
    That nets itself, as if of its own will.
The last thing chained Andromeda was thinking of
    Was how her tears might gain her some man's love!   430
Yet walking weeping and distraught at funerals can
    Seem most becoming to a brand new man.
Avoid the "cultured" man whose every hair in place
    Proclaims him just another pretty face:
He'll tell you what he's told a thousand girls in town;   435
    His errant "love" will never settle down.
And never love a man who's daintier than you;
    He may be fond of dainty fellows, too!
You won't believe me, but . . . believe (Troy would still be,
    Had it believed Cassandra's prophecy):   440
Liars will court you with a counterfeit of love,
    When wealth is all that they're desirous of.
But tresses dressed in shining nard are just a trick,
    While fussy toga-tucking's far too slick.
And don't be taken in by togas too fine-spun,   445
    Or flashy men who wear more rings than one
(The slickest of them all may be a thief who yearns
    To steal your finest clothes—for which he burns!).
"Give back what's mine!" fleeced women cry out in despair,
    "Give back what's mine!" resounding everywhere,   450

While Venus, from her temple radiant with gold,
    Looks down blasé, with Appian nymphs as cold.
And there are men of ill repute and known bad name
    Whose jilting of their lovers won them fame.
Learn from those jilted, so it won't occur again.   455
    And shut your door, for fear of lying men.
Athenian girls, don't trust in Theseus; once before,
    On all the gods he swears by now, he swore.
Demophoön, like Theseus, cannot be believed
    Now, since the day poor Phyllis was deceived.   460
In equal words, *good* promises should be repaid;
    With giving men, stick to the deal you've made.
(For it would take a girl who'd snuff a Vestal flame,
    Or rob an Io's relics without shame,
Or mix her man a wolfsbane-and-crushed-hemlock measure,   465
    To take his gifts and then deny him pleasure.)
And now let's get specific, Muse: rein in, and steer
    My chariot from too headlong a career.
Let words on tablets made of fir scout out the land,
    And careful serving maids take them in hand.   470
Inspect these notes; their words will tell you if he's true . . .
    Or if his "yearning soul" is duping you.
Then, stall awhile before you write; men *love* delay—
    As long as it's not longer than a day.
So don't concede too soon to an imploring youth,   475
    Yet don't be cruelly stingy with your ruth,
But make him fear *and* hope. Each time he writes, write back,
    To take him—just a little—off the rack.
Use comely words, but common, too: terms fine yet plain
    Enough to please the public, in the main.   480
Good notes will fire the timid man in certain cases,

While clumsy words can ruin pretty faces.
But since you also have a man to dupe—despite
    Your lack of any sacred marriage rite—
Have servants cut your letters (girl or boy), but just   485
    Be sure they go only to men you trust.
The worst men keep your every written scrap on hand
    For blackmail, wielding Aetna's firebrand.
I've seen girls pale with terror from this awful threat,
    Suffering agonies in fear's cold sweat.   490
So fighting fraud with fraud is fine with me, and so
    Is arming when you face an armored foe.
One hired hand to forge a dozen hands confuses
    (Oh, damn the men who drive me to such ruses!)
Nor is it safe inscribing wax you've not erased;   495
    You might find recent letters being traced.
I recommend you always call your lover "she"
    When writing; that's the best for secrecy.

Now let me turn from lesser things that scarce avail
    To greater matters filling out my sail.   500
Beauty should check its savage anger all it can;
    Rage is for beasts, but shining peace for man.
An angry face will swell as black veins burn and rise,
    And worse-than-Gorgon fire lights the eyes.
"No pipe's worth *that!*" puffed Pallas after she had caught her   505
    Own bloated image in the glassy water.
You ladies with a mirror: oh, if only you
    Could see your angry faces, you'd say, "*Who* . . . ?!"
And haughty looks will spoil your looks as well; I find
    That love requires glances that are kind.   510
(Believe an expert who abhors excessive pride;

In stony faces, seeds of hatred hide.)
Look back when he looks; smile when he smiles. Should he flirt,
    Begin a coy exchange. What could it hurt?
For that's when Cupid puts away the fencing steel   51
    And from his quiver, pulls the darts for real.
Let Ajax *have* Tecmessa. Grieving women bore me.
    I'm Roman, so the cheerful girls adore me!
I'd never ask Tecmessa or Andromache
    To be my mistress; no sad girls for me!   520
Without your children, who'd believe that either of you
    Had ever let a husband bed or love you?
Do you suppose she ever said to Ajax, "Dear,
    My Light," and other words men love to hear?

Now why should I not lead, and, leading, illustrate   525
    How little things can profit from the great?
Good generals assign their legions, cavalry,
    And eagles to the best man, naturally,
And so should you! Inspect us for what each does best,
    Then place us right and put us to the test.   530
Let rich men spoil you; lawyers, with their eloquence,
    Should plead your case and come to your defense.
But poets—well, expect no more than some fine verse;
    Where lovers are concerned, you *could* do worse.
Oh, far and wide, we give your dazzling beauty fame . . .   535
    And Nemesis and Cynthia a name.
Lycoris? Evening and the east both know her well,
    And "Who's Corinna"? many beg me tell.
Besides, the sacred poet sets no traps; his art
    Creates his character and honest heart.   540
He's not ambitious or in love with being paid,

But spurns the forum for the couch and shade.
We're caught quite easily, and burn with passion's heat,
　　Knowing the way to love without deceit.
Surely the placid art of verse will tend to render　　　　　545
　　Our ways and manners kind, our mores tender.
Be gentle, girls, with bards Aonian and Boeotian;
　　We have the Muses' numen and devotion.
In fact, our words go back and forth with gods, who speak,
　　Through poets, from Olympus' lofty peak.　　　　　550
Expecting gifts from learned poets is a crime—
　　Poor me!—girls love committing all the time.
So hide that greed; don't let it show. New lovers, seeing
　　The net you've laid, will spook, and soon be fleeing.
Use different bits if it's a hack the trainer trains,　　　　　555
　　Or some young colt who's never felt the reins.
So tracking down a youth is simply not the same
　　As making stable, older men your game.
So this raw boy, in Love's camp barely one whole day,
　　And knocking on your door to be your prey?　　　　　560
Make sure he knows no one but you; be sure he clings.
　　Then hedge that crop with high-grown poplar rings.
No rivals. When you're his alone, that's when you win.
　　Venus and kings don't share well; don't begin.
Wise veteran soldiers love, but suffer, bit by bit,　　　　　565
　　Some grief; a tyro won't put up with it.
(No battering of bedroom doors. No burning brands.
　　No raking of your cheeks with bloody hands.)
The older man won't rip your tunic . . . or his own.
　　No ravaged hair will make you weep or groan.　　　　　570
These are the works of boys so red-hot they've gone blind.
　　Campaigners suffer with a stoic mind.

Their fires smolder slowly like the hot damp hay—
    Like mountain saplings cut just yesterday.
Yes, *he's* the sure one; spurn the fecund younger man,   575
    And seize the fading fruit while you still can.

The gates are down, our secrets out, for good or ill,
    But in my faithless treason lies good will.
What's far too easy never nurtures love enough;
    Your pleasant love games need a rare rebuff.   580
So let him lie down at your door, crying, "Cruel door!"
    And threatening much (but pleading so much more).
The bitter salts our savor when the sweet displeases;
    Skiffs often sink, capsized by "perfect" breezes.
It's this that pushes bitter wives almost to breaking: 585
    Their husbands know they're there just for the taking.
Take one shut door and to it add a porter who
    Says, "No! You can't!" and love will touch you, too.
Now, stash away the kiddie-swords and pull the real.
    (No doubt, I'll be attacked by my own steel.)   590
Fresh lovers, when you've only now managed to net them,
    Think only *they* can find your bedroom. Let them.
Then later, let him sense a rival in your bed.
    (Ignore these arts, and love will soon be dead.)
The strong horse challenged by a peer who sets the pace   595
    Quickly outruns the field and wins the race.
A wrong revives love's fires banked for oh, so long.
    Myself? It's true: to love, I need a wrong.
But don't make obvious the cause of all his woes;
    Let him imagine far more than he knows.   600
A jealous man—or warder who does not exist—
    Should prove too much for young men to resist.

What good is pleasure when it's safe? No, even if
    You're free as Thaïs, you should act scared stiff!
So sneak him through the window though the coast is clear,   605
    And make your face the perfect mask of fear.
Rehearse your maid to burst in, crying, "We're undone!"
    Then hide the trembling boy; it should be fun!
Be sure to mix some pleasant sex in with the fear,
    Or he may bolt, never to re-appear.   610

I almost skipped the ways you can elude a keen-
    Eyed guard or husband who's both smart and mean.
Now, brides *should* fear their husbands; husbands, watch those brides!
    (So law or right or modesty provides.)
But closely guard the slave girl only lately freed?   615
    Unbearable! To cheat, study my creed.
Though guards add up like Argo's eyes, a steady will
    Will give them all the slip (it's not just skill).
Surely your guard can't stop your writing in the bath—
    That wash-up time in pleasure's aftermath?   620
How could he, when a confidante could carry writing
    Inside her bra so warm and so exciting?
When she could garter up most anything you wrote,
    Or slip beneath her sole your coaxing note?
But if he's wise to these, write letters on her back;   625
    She'll bear them like a weightless, secret pack.
Missives traced in fresh milk are safe and private, too;
    Sprinkling coal dust is all you need to do!
Or, just as good, the wet point of a fennel stalk
    Will make a dumb blank slate sit up and talk.   630
To guard his girl, Acrisius went to lots of bother,
    But still her sin made him someone's grandfather.

What can guards do, with theatres in so many places,
    And you still free to watch the chariot races,
Or shake the sistrum, praying to hear Isis low,   635
    Or go where merely male guards cannot go?
When Bona Dea won't let men observe her rites
    (Except for those she specially invites)?
When, even with the guards protecting clothes outside,
    So many baths have pleasures they can hide?   640
When any friend, as needed, gladly will pretend
    She's sick, then find a bed that she can lend?
What good are guards when dupes are made of keys *and* keys
    Make dupes, or windows let men in with ease?
When quantities of wine mean guardians can be lulled   645
    (Yes, even if it's Spanish grapes you've culled)?
And don't forget the drugs that make for darkest sleep,
    Drowning defeated eyes in Lethe's deep.
It's easy, too, to lull an odious guard with pleasures;
    Your maid just needs to take some lengthy measures!   650
But why digress on trivial tricks like these when one
    Small bribe should be enough to get it done?
Believe me: bribes can work with men *and* gods; why, even
    Great Jove responds to us when gifts are given.
When foolish men love bribes, what will the wise man do?   655
    With bribe in hand, he'll play the dummy, too.
But guards, once bought, must stay bought, on to God knows when,
    And be prepared to give and give again.
"Don't trust a friend," was my complaint once, and it's good
    For more than just the amorous brotherhood.   660
Too credulous, and other girls will seize your day;
    Don't let the hare you're hunting get away.
Be wary of the one who says, "Take *my* room—please,"

For we have often shared her bedroom keys.
And don't let pretty maids attend you; don't you see   665
    That they could play their mistress' part with me?

Naked before the foe, I write words that betray
    Myself! How I've gotten carried away!
No bird would show the fowler where his prey is found,
    No running deer instruct the hostile hound.   670
Let others play it safe—not me; I'll write on towards
    My goal, leaving my fate to Lemnian swords.
Convince us that we're loved (it's easy since we pray
    With pure desire; belief comes right away).
Look lovingly at your young man; sigh at your fate.   675
    Then ask him why he cruelly comes so late.
Let tears pile up about some "rival"; wail and weep
    Before grief makes you dig your nails in deep.
You'll have him then, and, quick to pity, he'll exclaim,
    "She loves me with pure passion's ardent flame!"   680
Especially if he's suave (his mirror's always kissed him),
    He's sure to think no goddess could resist him.
Whatever wrong he does, be only mildly cross;
    Don't let some "rival" put you at a loss.
For easy credence leads to harm; this you should know,   685
    Since Procris's example tells you so.

By blue hills of Hymettus, bright with blossoming,
    There lie a soft green grove and sacred spring.
Some modest trees compose this place, arbutus over
    Grasses, with laurel, rosemary, and clover.   690
Dense box tree leaves, domestic pine, fine tamarisk—
    All grow there. Myrtle scents the air, while brisk
And healthy breezes trade with zephyrs, swaying all

The varied leaves, and tree-tops shake in thrall.
This quiet spot pleased Cephalus, who sent away 695
    His men and dogs. Hunt-tired, down he lay.
And there he'd sing, "Come, fickle Aura, and relieve
    This heat; my body's ready to receive."
Some spying tattler told his wife (she'd conned each word),
    Informing timid ears just what she'd heard. 700
"My rival's Laura!" Such was Procris's belief,
    Who promptly fainted, mute with sudden grief.
She turned as pale as late leaves on the vine will turn
    When early winter frosts begin to burn;
As pale as quinces on the branches when they've hung 705
    Too long, or cornel cherries still too young.
Revived, she caught her flimsy dress and wildly tore
    It, then her blameless cheeks, which ran with gore.
At once, *she* ran in frenzy through the streets, hair streaming—
    A Bacchante goaded by a thyrsus, screaming. 710
And when she got there, Procris left her friends behind,
    Then, brave-but-stealthy, tip-toed to a blind.
Procris, while you stood hiding, what went through your mind?
    Inside your fiery heart, what did you find?
Oh, soon—not soon enough!—Laura would come, you thought, 715
    And then you'd see their shame, and they'd be caught!
Now pained to be there, and now pleased (that he'd be found
    Was not your wish), you spun your heart around.
The name, the place, the tale: you *must* believe! Besides,
    The mind believes in what it fears . . . and hides. 720
Seeing the flattened grass some recent body's pressed,
    She feels her heart jump in her fearful breast.
Thin shadows now contract as mid-day's hour comes on,
    And equidistant stand the dusk and dawn.
Back from the hunt, here's Hermes' son, perspiring. 725

He bathes his face with water from the spring
(While nervous Procris hides), then lies down with the prayer,
    "Come, *aura*; bring your soft reviving air."
Hearing this "name," sad Procris sees; her error's clear.
    Her wits return, as cheeks turn pink with cheer.   730
She rose, and rushing to her man to be embraced,
    Rustled the foliage that she displaced.
He, thinking her some beast, leapt up, a young man ready,
    And in his right hand held his weapon steady.
No, wretched Cephalus, she's not some prey! Don't do   735
    It! Oh, too late: your lance has pierced her through.
"My Love," she cries. "To shoot a true and tender heart!
    You've always found a way to wound this part
Of me. I die before my day, but rival-free,
    Which means the earth will lightly lie on me.   740
My breath expires in the air I feared once; close
    My eyelids with your dear hand as it goes!"
Grieving, he takes her lifeless form to heart and sears
    The oh-so-cruel wound with scalding tears.
She dies, and breath-by-breath, he takes what was her life   745
    Upon his lips, kissing his reckless wife.

But back to work now; back to barest facts to get
    This tired craft to port (it's not there yet).
So now you want my good advice because you're nervous
    About how parties work? I'm at your service.   750
First hint: come last ... or late; low light can charm by fraud
    When girls come late and lateness plays the bawd.
Though ugly, you'll seem beautiful to those who drink,
    And night will hide more faults than you may think.
Take up your food by fingertip; form counts at table.   755

(And keep your face as clean as you are able.)
Don't gorge at home, but try to eat less than you could
    Once at the party; cramming won't look good.
Had Paris seen his Helen stuffing up her face,
    He'd have despised her: "She's a vile disgrace."   760
Drinking becomes a girl the best; you are a joy,
    Bacchus, when partying with Venus' boy.
Now ... when the head stays clear, both mind and feet remain
    Steady—no seeing double in your brain.
A wine-soaked girl invites the worst abuse, which serves   765
    Her right; she gets the sex that she deserves.
Nor is it safe to sleep when all the wine is gone;
    So much that's shameful could be going on.

I blush to teach what follows, but ... hear Venus chide,
    "In blushing matters, I'm your special guide."   770
Ladies should know their bodies, choosing what is best
    For them; one manner may not fit the rest.
If you're another pretty face, then lie back flat;
    But if your back's the charm, then show him that.
Milanion set Atalanta's legs to rest   775
    Around his neck; do your legs pass the test?
You little women, "ride the horse." Poor Hector's wife,
    Too tall, could never ride him all her life.
If your long legs look good, then make the most of it;
    Kneel on the bed, your neck bent back a bit.   780
With youthful thighs, and breasts fault-free, you ought to lie
    Slant-wise across the bed; have *him* stand by.
Like some Thessalian mother, let your hair fly free;
    Toss back your head so men can clearly see.
Lucina may have written on your flesh, of course.   785

If so, play Parthian; turn around your horse.
Love's thousand modes! Here's one that's easy on the spine:
    Try lying right-side down, semi-supine.
But neither horny Ammon nor Apollo sings
    You truer words than those my own Muse brings.   790
If you can trust an art I've practiced hard and long,
    Believe me and the good faith of my song.
Deep down, the woman should feel wrung by venery—
    An act to please both sexes equally.
Don't stint on teasing talk; on moaning, purring, humming;   795
    In sex play, keep the less-than-proper coming.
And that *includes* the girl so frigid she can't feel;
    Cry out with joy—even if it's not real.
(It's sad when in that special place [I *don't* mean bed]
    Where couples ought to share, the girl is dead.)   800
But when you fake it, don't be obvious; compel
    Belief with rolling eyes, so he can't tell.
To prove you're satisfied, let words and panting show.
    (Too bad our parts have secret signals, though!)
The girl who begs a small "gift" moments after sex   805
    Is *not* about to get what she expects.
And by the way: keep windows shut—too much clear light,
    When bodies should be mostly out of sight.

Our revels now are ended. Swans whose necks were bending
    To draw us on, now halt. Time for descending.   810
As young men marked their trophies once before, just so
    The girls now: "Naso taught us all we know."

NOTES

❦

Translator's Preface

1 Sarah Funke Butler, "Document: Nabokov's Notes," *Paris Review Daily*, February 29, 2012: "Nabokov stated that he had begun work on a second, revised edition, [of *Eugene Onegin*] to be 'even more gloriously and monstrously literal than the first'; he felt that his first edition was 'still not close enough and not ugly enough. In future editions . . . I think I shall turn it entirely into utilitarian prose, with a still bumpier brand of English, rebarbative barricades of square brackets and tattered banners of reprobate words, in order to eliminate the last vestiges of bourgeois poesy and concession to rhythm. This is something to look forward to. For the moment, all I wish is merely to put on record my utter disgust with the general attitude, amoral and Philistine, towards literalism.'"

2 Gail M. Gerhart, Review of Adam Hochschild, *King Leopold's Ghost: A Story of Greed, Terror, and Heroism in Colonial Africa, Foreign Affairs* (March/April 1999). Joseph Conrad's novel *Heart of Darkness* also deals with this history, brilliantly.

3 John Dryden, "Preface" to *Ovid's Epistles*, 1680.

4 Charles Martin, "A Classic in Paraphrase," *Blackbird* (Fall 2010).

5 Lord Byron (George Gordon Noel, Lord Byron), "The Destruction of Sennacherib," *Occasional Pieces*, 1807–1824.

Amores

BOOK I

Epigram
The first edition of the *Amores* is lost.

I.1

1–4   "Prepared for war": The speaker claims to have been dissuaded from *epic verse*, which he would have written in dactylic hexameter (six feet of three syllables each—long, short, short), to *love elegy*, composed in couplets of six and five feet.

12–15   Mars; Aonian; Helicon: Mars is the Roman god of war. Aonia, in Greece, is the site of Mt. Helicon, home to the Muses. Hence, "lyre."

20   "or boy": The speaker claims he cannot write erotic verse about boys.

29   "myrtle": The sacred flower of Venus.

30   "Eleven-footed Muse of Elegy": The elegiac couplet comprises eleven feet. Here, Elegy (personified) serves as the speaker's muse.

I.2

5   Love: Cupid (Amor; Eros)

24   "mother's pigeon pair": Venus's chariot is drawn by doves.

45   "blind seer": Cupid was often depicted as blindfolded.

51   "cousin Caesar's": Augustus, Ovid's emperor, was thought to be descended, through Julius Caesar, from Aeneas and Venus (Aeneas founded Rome).

I.3

21   "she who turned/Bovine": Io was turned into a cow by Juno, Jove's jealous wife.

22   "one a swan": Leda, raped by Jove in the form of a swan, gave birth to Helen of Troy.

23   "that girl": Europa, swept out to sea by Jove in the form of a bull.

I.4

7   "Atrax's daughter"; "half-men": Hippodamia's wedding to Pirithous degenerated into a brawl between Lapiths and Centaurs. The half-men were Centaurs (part horse). Atrax was Hippodamia's father.

30   "the ganymede": Ganymede was the cup-bearer to Zeus. The name became synonymous with the generic office.

I.6

71   Parthian: Because it is a last-second comment, hurled as the speaker retreats—a "Parthian shot." The Parthians ruled in eastern Persia from about 250 B.C.E., and their archers shot their arrows from horseback, in retreat—from which, corrupted, comes "parting shot."

I.7

9 "Agamemnon's son": Orestes, who avenged his father Agamemnon's death by killing his adulterous mother Clytemnestra. Aeschylus and Euripides both treat the subject in plays.

31 "Tydeus' son": Diomede, who wounded Venus during the Trojan war.

51 Parian: The Greek island of Paros was famed for its marble.

I.8

2 Dipsas: "Thirsty."

4 "Memnon's mother": Aurora, goddess of the dawn.

39–40 "Sabine women...Tatius": Titus Tatius, king of the Sabines, joined with Romulus to rule Rome after the rape of the Sabine women.

50 "Heraclitean": The Greek philosopher (fl. 515 B.C.E.) taught that one could not step into the same river twice.

64 "Chalked feet": Newly imported slaves were marked by chalking their feet.

67 "Adonises": Adonis was a mythical young man loved by Venus and famous for his beauty.

I.9

2 Atticus: We do not know whether this was a real person.

34 Argive: Another epithet for the Greek forces; "from Argos."

39–40 "Mars...known": Vulcan threw a fine-meshed net over the bed containing his adulterous wife and the amorous Mars. The gods came to watch and laugh.

I.10

1 Phrygian; Eurotas: "Trojan." The Eurotas is a river in Laconia, in Greece. Paris, the Trojan prince, seduced and ran off with Helen, queen of Sparta and wife of Menelaus, thus starting the Trojan war. Hence, her "dual husbands' wars."

49–50 Sabine; Tarpeia: The legendary Tarpeia threw open the gates of Rome to the Sabine army, demanding as her price "what they wore on their arms"—gold cuffs. They killed her with the weight of the shields they bore. The Tarpeian rock was the execution site for Roman traitors.

51–52 "Or one...lavaliere": Alcmaeon killed his mother Eriphyle because she sent his father Amphiaraus to die in the war of the Seven Against Thebes. The Seven's leader, Polynices, had bribed her with a golden necklace.

I.11

1 Napê: We do not know whether this was a real person.

25 bay: Bay leaf (laurel); the crown of victory.

I.12

9 hemlock: A poisonous herb.

10 "Corsican…die": Corsican honey was famously bitter.

27 "like your name": Diptych; hence, two "wings."

I.13

1 "her old husband"; Dawn: Aurora was pictured driving a chariot across the sky. Her husband was Tithonus, condemned to age forever.

3–4 "Memnon's rites": Aurora's son Memnon died at Troy, killed by Achilles. Apparently (Ovid is our only source for this myth), birds were thought to rise from his ashes on the anniversary of his death and fight a kind of battle over his tomb.

31–32 Ethiop: Tithonus was Ethiopian. The speaker of the poem imagines him to be dark-skinned. Hence, his "black shade."

43–44 "Jove…way": Jove disguised himself as Alcmene's husband Amphitryon, then impregnated her. She gave birth to Hercules (Herakles). Apparently, two nights were needed by the ruler of the gods to pull off this ruse.

I.14

39 Thessalian: Thessaly, northeast of Greece, its coastline bordering the Aegean Sea.

49 Sygambrian: The Sygambri, a Germanic tribe, were defeated by Rome in 11 B.C.E. Their shorn hair was made into wigs.

I.15

9 "Maeonia's"; Tenedos: Homer was thought to be from Maeonia. Tenedos, an island off the coast of Asia Minor, figures prominently in the *Aeneid*.

11 "Ascraean Hesiod": Hesiod (fl. 700 B.C.E.) wrote the *Theogony* and *Works and Days*, poems on the birth of the gods and on the means to living an honest life, respectively. He came from Ascra in Greece.

22 Aesonian: Of or related to Aeson, Thessalian father of Jason, principal hero of the quest for the Golden Fleece.

BOOK II

II.1

1 "Paelignian": The Paeligni were a tribe of central Italy, in the Abruzzi.

23–24 Luna; Sol: The moon and the sun. Ovid is alluding to the magic powers of verse.

29 "Achilles' speed": The hero was famous for his speed afoot.

II.2

1 Bagoas: A conventional (Persian) name for a eunuch.

4 "Danaus's girls": Danaus, king of Argos, had 50 daughters, all of which, except Hypermnestra, killed their husbands on their wedding night.

II.4

15 "Sabine-cold": The Sabine women were proverbial for their austere virtue.

II.5

39 Lydian: From Asia Minor, directly opposite Greece across the Aegean Sea.

II.6

15 "Pylades and Agamemnon's son": Orestes and Pylades were famous for their friendship.

22 "Punic-red": Tyre, in Phoenicia (hence "Punic"), was well known for its red-pink dyes.

35 raven; Minerva: The goddess punished the bird for gossiping by turning it black.

38 "gifted…Ganges": Presumably the bird is a gift brought from India.

49 Elysian: The Elysian Fields were the paradise of the underworld.

53 "Bird of Fire": The Phoenix, a mythical bird that rose to new life from its funeral ashes.

II.7

3 "marble gods": "The gods" is a Britishism for a mezzanine or gallery, presumably from its height and distance from the "earthly" floor below.

II.8

11–12 "Achilles…woe": The hero claimed Briseis, captured at Troy, for his own. Agamemnon demanded her from the hero because the Greek leader had yielded up Chryseis.

II.9a

7–8 "Achilles...surgeon": Achilles was supposed to have healed the wound of his own victim, Telephus, with rust from his spear.

22 "sword...sign": A retired gladiator was presented with a wooden sword, the *rudis*. A *rudis* figures slightly in the plot of the movie *Gladiator*.

II.11

3–5 Colchis; "crashing rocks": Colchis lay on the far eastern shore of the Black (Euxine) Sea, home of the Golden Fleece. The rocks were the Symplegades, at the Bosporus, the Black Sea's entrance. When Jason, sailing the *Argo* in search of the fleece, successfully negotiated these obstacles, they ceased to clash forever.

20 "Syrtes' sandbars": Off North Africa. Famous for their danger.

29 "halcyon...twins": Halcyone, grieving her drowned husband Ceyx, was transformed into a bird, as was he. For seven days before and after the winter solstice, the winds are calm and safe for sailors, as Halcyone is said to be brooding on her nest. Hence, "halcyon days" as an allusion to calm and peaceful weather. Leda's twins are Castor and Pollux, the Dioscuri, associated with St. Elmo's fire—the blue light that appears on a ship's mast, and that the Romans considered a good omen in a storm.

44 "gods": It is not clear from the Latin if the speaker means his household gods or some other figures placed on, or carved into, the ship's stern.

II.12

17 casus belli: A cause or occasion of war.

21–22 "Someone's wife...war": Lavinia was promised as a bride to Aeneas, the founder of Rome, by her father Latinus. The disconcerted suitor Turnus then went to war with Aeneas.

23–24 "Brides...young": Romulus, the eponymous founder of Rome, contrived to have the Roman men abduct the Sabine women for their brides. War followed.

II.13

11 sistrum: A rattle used in the cult of Isis.

II.14

11–12 "some pair...grow": Deucalion and Pyrrha survived the great flood that destroyed mankind. They repopulated the earth by throwing stones backwards over their shoulders, thus "seeding" a new generation of human beings. Ovid tells the story in the *Metamorphoses*.

13–14 "mother of / Achilles": Thetis, a sea nymph or Nereid. She hid the infant Achilles to save him.

17 "Venus...Aeneas": Aeneas was Venus's child by Anchises, a Trojan shepherd. Aeneas carrying his father Anchises on his back out of the wreckage of Troy was a favorite motif of ancient and renaissance painters.

18 "orphan...Caesars": The emperor Augustus claimed to trace his ancestry all the way back to Aeneas.

II.16

14 "The Twins": Castor and Pollux.

24 "Malea's...cape": A famously dangerous promontory on the southeastern coast of Greece.

31 Leander; Hero: Legendary lovers. Leander swam the Hellespont to reach Hero, but drowned one night in the attempt. Hero then killed herself from grief.

39 Scythian: Scythia lay beyond the Black Sea.

II.17

17 Egeria: Egeria was wife to Numa Pompilius, second king of Rome.

24 "Forum advocate": Lawyers pled their cases in the Forum.

II.18

1 Macer: A real person, Pompeius Macer, poet friend of Ovid, and the Emperor Augustus's director of Rome's libraries.

18 "buskined bard": Actors wore high boots (the buskin or *cothurnus*).

22–26 "Phyllis's...Sappho": A long series of abandoned women who in Ovid's epistolary poems the *Heroides* wrote letters to their faraway husbands or lovers. Phyllis, betrothed to Demophoon, son of the Thracian king, committed suicide when the young soldier sailed off to Cyprus. Paris deserted Oenone, a river nymph, for Helen of Troy. Macareus conceived an incestuous passion for his sister Canace. The siblings' father was Aeolus, god of the winds. On his quest for the Golden Fleece, Jason abandoned the Lemnian queen Hypsipyle after begetting two children with her. Hippolytus, son of Theseus, spurned the amorous advances of his stepmother Phaedra. Theseus himself abandoned Ariadne on the island of Naxos even after she had helped him defeat the Minotaur. Dido, the Carthaginian queen who helped Aeneas, was deserted by him so that he might found Rome. She then committed suicide. Sappho, the seventh-century B.C.E. poet of Lesbos, attracted a number of legendary stories, including her supposedly suicidal passion for Phaon, who left her and went to Sicily.

BOOK III

III.1

8   "One foot…short": Elegiac verse consists of couplets of six and five feet, respectively.

24   "Bacchus…wand": The *thyrsis*.

53   "hung": As love elegy, the written poem is imagined as having been nailed to doorposts.

59   "stylus": The instrument used to incise the wax tablets on which the poet wrote.

III.2

1   "for the horses": The scene imagined is the chariot races.

16   "Pisaean spear": "Pisaean" because Oenomaus's kingdom was Pisa, on the Alpheus river in Elis.

44   "parade": Before the race, there occurred a procession of images of the gods.

54   "boxers, Pollux": Pollux's Greek name was Polydeuces; he was a renowned pugilist.

66   praetor: The official who signaled the start of the race.

73   "Quirites: re-call!": The common Roman citizen was *quiris*. By throwing his toga, the spectator could demand a re-start of the race.

III.5

Some scholars believe this allegorical poem is not Ovid's, though it appears in some manuscripts.

III.6

39–42   Nile; Euanthe; Asopus: The myth is obscure.

47–66   "Ilia…earn": Seduced by Mars, the Vestal Virgin Ilia was sentenced to death by drowning in the Anio. The river god pitied her and saved her. She is "Idaean" because of her descent from Aeneas, who lived near Mt. Ida (near Troy).

76   "Trojan altar fires": Her home deities, brought from Troy.

III.7

8   Sithonian: Thracian.

III.8

9–10   "knight…bloodshed": A battlefield promotion to the Equestrian class.

30   "become a shower": In visiting Danaë.

35 "Saturn reigned": The Golden Age—the "good old days," when Saturn and the Titans ruled, not Zeus.

48 onager: A siege catapult (the word refers to a wild ass).

III.9

15–16 Venus…Adonis: The goddess fell in love with the handsome young man, who was later killed by a boar he had wounded.

21 "Ismarian Orpheus…song": Mt. Ismarus, in Thrace, was the home of the great musician Orpheus, whose art could tame wild beasts and move stones.

25 Maeonian: Lydian. Homer's birthplace was thought to be Lydia.

26 Pierian: "Of the Muses." Pieria lay in Macedonia. Pieros was the father of the nine Muses.

30 "the sheet…restore": To fend off her suitors, Penelope, having promised to choose one of them after finishing her father-in-law's burial shroud she was weaving by day, would secretly undo the work at night.

III.10

19 "Cretans…true": Cretans were considered notorious liars in antiquity.

20 "raised…due": Jove was hidden away as an infant on Crete, where the people raised him.

III.12

15 Thebes; Troy; Caesar: Possible subjects for "serious" epic poems.

23 "Winged…hair": Traditional features of these mythological beings.

29 "wineskin…wind": Odysseus received from Aeolus a bag or wineskin containing all the winds. His curious crew opened the wineskin…with disastrous results.

31 "bears…sky": Callisto, the bear constellation set in the sky by a jealous Juno.

35 "dragon teeth…seed": When Cadmus killed a dragon at Thebes, he sowed the beast's teeth in the earth to grow a "crop" of fighting men.

36 "cattle…breed": Medea's father Aeëtes ordered Jason to yoke a pair of fire-breathing bulls.

38 "nymphs…ships": An episode in the *Aeneid*, Book IX.

39 "Atreus's meal": Atreus killed his brother Thyestes' children, then served them to their father at a banquet.

40 "rocks…feel": Amphion, the skilled musical son of Zeus, played the lyre so beautifully that the stones of Thebes assembled themselves to its strains.

III.13

19–20   "Goat...begun": A textual crux. No one but Ovid seems ever to have heard of this story.

26   palla: A woman's long robe.

27–35   "Greek forebears...rite": Learned poets of Ovid's temperament loved to invent playful etymological foundation stories such as these (Halaesus>Halisca>Falisca).

III.14

11   Rumor: A personified force of considerable power.

44   meretrix: A Roman female who earned her living by the selling of sexual favors. Hence, the word *meretricious*.

III.15

10   "the Social War": From 91 to 87 B.C.E., Rome's Italian allies fought against the city (they were, otherwise, the *socii*). Rome granted her opponents citizenship at war's end, thus securing Italo-Roman unity.

15   Amathusian: Amathus was a city on the coast of Cyprus, the island sacred to Venus.

Ars Amatoria

BOOK I

4   Amor: The god of love, also called Eros, Cupid, and Love.

6   Tiphys; Haemonian: Tiphys piloted the *Argo* in search of the Golden Fleece. The ship was Haemonian in that many of the Golden Fleece heroes were from Thessaly, or Haemonia, on the northeast coast of Greece.

28   "old Hesiod's": Greek poet (fl. 700 B.C.E.) who wrote the *Theogony* and *Works and Days*.

53   Perseus; Andromeda: The hero and the maiden he rescued from a sea monster.

57   "Methymnian"; "Gargarian": Roughly, Lesbian; Methymnia was a city on the island's northwest coast. Gargara was a crest of Mt. Ida.

67   "Pompey's portico"; Sol: Gnaeus Pompeius Magnus (106–48 B.C.E.), Julius Caesar's rival, had a colonnade built in 55 B.C.E. in the southern area of the Campus Martius; Sol = the sun.

71   "Empress Livia's": Livia Drusilla (58 B.C.E.–C.E. 29), wife of the Emperor Augustus and mother of the Emperor Tiberius.

73   "Apollo's temple"; "Belus' daughters": probably the Temple Apolla Palatinus, on Rome's Palatine hill; Belus' 50 granddaughters, the Danaides, married then killed his 50 grandsons.

77   "Io's temple": Seduced by Zeus, Io was turned into a cow by Hera, Zeus's wife.

82   Appian: the Appian Way, a major Roman street.

102   "Sabine rapes": Under Romulus, the Romans carried off and married the women of the Sabini (northeast of Rome) and thus populated the city.

111   Tuscan: Etruscan; of the indigenous peoples of pre-Roman Italy; roughly, the region around modern-day Florence.

163   Forum: Rome's principal public square.

171   "Caesar . . . sea-fight": The Emperor Augustus commanded this re-enactment of the battle of Salamis, fought between Greece and Persia, in 2 B.C.E.

178   "our Pax": the famous Pax Romana, or Roman Peace.

179   Parthia: roughly, northern Persia, along the eastern shore of the Caspian Sea.

180   "our eagles": The symbols atop the standards of the Roman legions.

181   "young Gaius": Gaius Caesar (20 B.C.E.–C.E. 4), Augustus's grandson.

187   Tirynthian: Hercules' birthplace was the Argolid city of Tiryns.

220   "stream's . . . float?": Conquered peoples and kingdoms were paraded in the Roman triumph.

223–224   Euphrates; Tigris: Rivers in modern-day Iraq.

225   Armenians: A people living between the Black and Caspian Seas.

255   "Baiae by the bay": A famous pleasure-resort on the coast south of Rome.

272   Arcadian: roughly, Greek.

293   "Cydonia's . . . Crete": Cydonia is a city in northwest Crete.

327   "Aerope . . . Thyestes": A Cretan princess, Aerope married the Greek king Atreus, but committed adultery with his brother Thyestes.

335   "Creusa . . . Ephyre": New wife to Jason (after Medea), she was burned to death by a poison robe sent by Medea; Ephyre is the ancient name for Corinth.

337   "Amyntor's Phoenix": Amyntor's mistress Phthia accused his son Phoenix of seducing her.

405   Kalends: The first day of the Roman month.

507   "Magna Mater singers": The eunuch-priests of the Asian goddess Cybele.

508   Phrygian: Phrygia was a region of central modern-day Turkey. Also a musical scale or mode.

541　Bacchants: Maenads.

558　Cretan Crown: the constellation Aurora Borealis.

563　Hymenaeus: God of weddings and marriages (also "Hymen").

565　Dionysian: Dionysus = Bacchus.

585–588　These lines may be spurious—a later editor's addition.

625　Juno; Minerva: The Roman Hera and Athena respectively; Zeus's wife and daughter.

653　"Perillus . . . Phalaris": Lines 653–654 explain themselves.

679　"Phoebe's . . . rapist": Daughter of Leucippus, Phoebe was carried off by Castor. Her sister Hilaira suffered the same fate at the hands of Pollux.

681　"girl from Scyros": Deidameia, daughter of Lycomedes; seduced/raped by Achilles.

BOOK II

56　"Virgin Bear": Constellation of the nymph Callisto, who was transformed into Ursa Major.

102　"Marsian charms": Italian tribe (the Marsi) noted for their spells and magic.

150　"Chaonian doves . . . towers": On the northwest coast of Greece, Chaonia was known for these oracular birds.

183　"Numidian": Numidia is roughly modern-day Algeria.

193　"Maenalus's slope": Mountain in the heart of the Peloponnese.

219　"Ionian": Ionia is a region on the central west coast of modern-day Turkey.

297　Tyrian: of Tyre, city on the Phoenician coast; it was noted for its purple dyes.

298　"Coan silk": Aegean island (Cos) famous for this fabric.

381　"Phasian . . . Jason": Phasis was a town (and river) in the Colchis, home of Medea; Jason was the Argonaut who won the Golden Fleece.

383　"Procne's": Learning of her sister Philomela's rape by King Tereus, she served him his own son Itys in revenge, then fled, turning into a swallow.

423　"Hymettian honey": Mt. Hymettus (southeast of Athens) was famed for its honey.

491　"Machaon's juices": Machaon was physician to the Greek army at Troy.

541　"Dodonian oaks": Zeus's oracular trees at Dodona, in Epirus, on the northwest coast of Greece.

658 "Illyrian tar": Illyria was the northwest region of the Balkan peninsula, on the eastern Adriatic Sea.

669–674 Most scholars believe these lines belong after line 732, where I have placed them.

BOOK III

1 Amazons: Women warriors, allies of Troy.

37–38 Nine Ways; Phyllis: Amphipolis, in Thrace, where Phyllis went down to the sea to look for Demophöon nine times; he had deserted her.

83 Latmos; Luna; Endymion: Luna, the moon goddess (also "Selene"), ensconced her beloved mortal Endymion on Mt. Latmos in southwest Turkey.

147 Cyllenian: Mt. Cyllene lies west of Corinth.

155 Iole; Alcides: Oechalian princess of Thessaly, courted by Hercules ("Alcides").

176 "Ino's Phrixus . . . Helle": Their stepmother Ino tried to kill the twins Phrixus and Helle, but they were rescued by a flying golden ram. Helle fell off into the sea, bequeathing her name to the Hellespont.

244 Bona Dea: (the "good goddess" in Latin); her cult was Italian, and was meant to protect the Roman people.

270 Pharian: Of the Egyptian island Pharos, at the mouth of the Nile; famous for its lighthouse.

304 Umbrian: Umbria = central Italy.

321 "Rhodopian Orpheus": great musician whose skill could move rocks and trees; the Rhodopian range lay in southern Thrace.

322 "Tartarus' three-headed cur": Cerberus, guard-dog of the underworld, of which Tartarus was the deepest region.

346 "letter-poems . . . begin": Ovid's Heroides are poems in the form of letters written by wives and lovers to their absent spouses, lovers, and betrayers.

385 "the Maid": The Aqua Virgo, a Roman aqueduct famed for its cold water.

388 "Virgo's flaming": Virgo = the constellation ascendant from mid-August to mid-September.

391 "Octavia's . . . arcades": Roman porticoes named after the Emperor Augustus's sister and wife respectively.

463 "Vestal flame": Vesta, goddess of the hearth; the flame in her temple had to be kept going since it symbolized the life of Rome.

547   Aonian; Boeotian: The terms are roughly interchangeable, Boeotia being the coast of Greece lying across from the island Euboea.

672   Lemnian: Lemnos's women, afflicted with the punishment of a sickening smell by Aphrodite because they would not honor her, killed their husbands, who had imported new wives from Thrace.

GLOSSARY

Accius: Accius (170–86 B.C.E.) was both a poet and literary scholar. He had something of a reputation for getting back at his rivals and enemies. Hence, "tart of tongue."

Achaia: Roughly, Greece.

Achelous [Hercules; Calydon; Aetolia; Deianira]: The (horned) river god Achelous, of Aetolia, fought with Hercules for the hand of Deianira. In the struggle, the god lost a piece of his horns. Deianira's father ruled Calydon.

Achilles: Preeminent Greek warrior whose wrath is the subject of the *Iliad*.

Acrisius: Father of Danaë. Raped by Zeus, Danaë gave birth to Acrisius's grandson, Perseus.

Admetus: Thessalian king loved by Apollo, who in the form of a mortal tended his cattle.

Adonis: A handsome young man loved by Venus, he died and turned into an anemone. Shakespeare's narrative poem tells the story, as does Ovid in his *Metamorphoses*, Book X.

Aegisthus: Thyestes's son and Clytemnestra's adulterous lover.

Aeneas: Child of Venus by Anchises, a Trojan shepherd, he is the hero of Virgil's foundation epic the *Aeneid*.

Aerope [Thyestes]: A Cretan princess, she married the Greek king Atreus, but committed adultery with his brother Thyestes.

Aeson: Thessalian father of Jason, who was the principal hero of the quest for the Golden Fleece.

Agamemnon: Greek leader at Troy who was murdered by his wife Clytemnestra on his return home.

Ajax: Greek hero who, failing to win the armor of the dead Achilles at Troy, went mad, destroying flocks of sheep.

Alcestis [Admetus]: A Greek princess, daughter of Pelias, she gave up her life for Admetus, dying in his place.

Alcinous: Phaeacian king famous for his wealth—especially his orchards.

Allia: River where Rome was defeated by the Gauls in 390 B.C.E.

Alpheus [Arethusa; Arcadia]: From Arcadia, in central Greece, the river Arethusa fled the river Alpheus. She flowed underground and reappeared in Sicily.

Amaryllis: The lover of Virgil's shepherd Corydon in the *Eclogues*.

Amathus: City on the coast of Cyprus, the island sacred to Venus.

Ammon: Horned Egyptian god roughly comparable to Zeus.

Amphion: The skilled musical son of Zeus, he played the lyre so beautifully that the stones of Thebes assembled themselves to its strains.

Amphipolis: Place in Thrace where Phyllis went down to the sea to look for Demophöon nine times; he had deserted her.

Amyclae: City in southern Sparta, site of a temple to Apollo.

Amymone: Daughter of Danaus. Neptune raped her as she went to draw water.

Amyntor [Phoenix]: Amyntor's mistress Phthia accused his son Phoenix of seducing her.

Anacreon: A lyric poet of Teos (fl. 540 B.C.E.), noted for his drinking songs.

Andromache: The wife of the great Trojan prince and hero Hector.

Andromeda: The virgin daughter of King Cepheus of Ethiopia, she was chained to a rock as a sacrifice to the sea monster ravaging the coast. Perseus killed the monster and won Andromeda for his bride.

Anio [Tibur]: The river Anio forms waterfalls at Tibur (modern-day Tivoli).

Anubis: Egyptian god who conducts souls to the afterlife.

Aonia [Boeotia]: The terms are roughly interchangeable, Boeotia being the coast of Greece lying across from the island Euboea.

Apelles: Famous Greek painter (fl. 330 B.C.E.).

Apis: Sacred bull of Egypt. The soul or life of Osiris was believed to have passed into him. He was closely associated with the Nile.

Aratus: Greek poet of astronomy (fl. 280 B.C.E.).

Argo: Mythical ship on which Greek heroes sailed to find the Golden Fleece.

Argus: A hundred-eyed monster, he was stationed to guard Io, one of Zeus's many loves. The creature was later killed by Hermes (Mercury), and his eyes removed and placed in the tail of the peacock, Hera's sacred bird.

Ariadne: The princess of Crete; she fell in love with the Athenian hero Theseus and helped him kill the monster called the Minotaur, but was then deserted by him.

Arion: A musician who escaped pirates by jumping overboard and was rescued by a dolphin.

Armenia: A land between the Black and Caspian Seas.

Ascanius: The son of Aeneas.

Asopus: A river in Boeotia, in Greece.

Astypalaea: An Aegean island southeast of Naxos.

Atalanta: A fleet-footed maiden who outran all her suitors but Melanion, who tricked her by rolling golden apples in her course. Atalanta made the mistake of stopping to gather them.

Athos [Hybla]: A sacred mountain on the Thessalonian peninsula. Hybla, a town in southern Sicily, was a byword for honey.

Atlas: A mythological figure who held the heavens on his back.

Atrides: The sons and descendants of Atreus, i.e., Agamemnon and Menelaus, Greek leaders of the forces at Troy.

Aura: In Latin, "breeze," but mistaken by Procris for a woman's name ("Laura"). Ovid tells the story in his *Metamorphoses*, Book VII.

Auster: The South Wind.

Automedon: Achilles's charioteer.

Avernus: A lake in the underworld.

Bacchus: The Roman equivalent of the Greek Dionysus, he was born of Semele and Zeus. The object of numerous cults, he is the god of (among other things) wine.

Bagoas: A conventional (Persian) name for a eunuch.

Baiae: A famous pleasure-resort on the coast south of Rome.

Bona Dea: In Latin, "the good goddess." Her cult was Italian, and was meant to protect the Roman people.

Boreas: The North Wind, he raped Orithyia, daughter of the legendary king of Athens, Erectheus.

Briseis: Girl taken by Agamemnon from Achilles to compensate for the loss of Chryseis.

Byblis: Mythological woman who fell in love with her brother Caunus. Ovid tells the story in his *Metamorphoses*, Book IX.

Caicus: A river in Mysia, an area northwest of Troy.

Callimachus: An elegant, ironic, learned Greek poet of Alexandria (fl. 260 B.C.E.).

Calypso: An enchantress in the *Odyssey*. Her charms held the hero for seven years before he set sail for his home of Ithaca.

Cassandra: A princess of Troy, and later captive mistress of Agamemnon. She was fated never to be believed despite her gift of accurate prophecy.

Catullus [Calvus]: Love poets and friends of Tibullus's. Catullus: 84–54 B.C.E.

Calvus: 82–47 B.C.E.

Caucasus (the): Mountain range between the Black and Caspian Seas.

Cephalus: Attic hunter abducted by Eos ("Dawn").

Cepheis: Another name for Andromeda (her father was Cepheus).

Ceraunia: The "Thunder Mountains" of Epirus, in northwestern Greece.

Cerberus: The three-headed guard-dog of the underworld.

Ceres: Goddess of grain and crops.

Cerina: Latin for "waxen."

Chaonia: Land on the northwest coast of Greece, known for its oracular birds.

Chiron: A centaur (half man, half horse), he tutored the great Greek warrior Achilles.

Chlide [Pitho; Libas]: Chlide means "naughtiness," Pitho "persuasion," and Libas "little river." These are courtesans' nicknames.

Chryses: Agamemnon, forced by Apollo's plague on the Greeks at Troy, returned the girl Chryseis to her father, the priest Chryses.

Cilicia: A land in southern Asia Minor.

Circe: The sorceress of the *Odyssey*. Her magic turned Odysseus's men into animals.

Circus: The Circus Maximus, built by Julius Caesar and located between the Aventine and Palatine hills.

Clio: The Muse of history.

Clotho: One of the three Fates, she holds the staff from which the thread of human life is spun.

Cnossus: A city in Crete that was the site of the royal palace.

Corinna: Ovid's (notional?) mistress in the *Amores*.

Cos: An Aegean island noted for its silk.

Creusa: The new wife of Jason (after Medea), she was burned to death by a poisoned robe sent by Medea.

Cupid: The god of love as physical desire. The son of Venus, he strikes his victims with arrows. Also called Eros and Amor.

Cydippe: Tricked into marrying Acontius by the gift of an apple that bore the words, "I swear by Artemis that I will marry Acontius," she read the words aloud, as was the classical custom, and was trapped.

Cydnus: The river Tarsus, in southern Turkey.

Cydonia: City in northwest Crete.

Cyllene: Mountain west of Corinth.

Cypassis: Corinna's maid and hairdresser. She would have been a slave.

Daedalus: A master craftsman and inventor who with his son Icarus escaped from Crete on man-made wings. Icarus flew too near the sun, and the wax that held the wings together melted. He died falling into the Icarian Sea, which was named after him.

Danaë: She was courted in her brazen tower by Zeus in the form of a shower of gold.

Danaus: The king of Argos, he had 50 daughters, all of whom, except Hypermnestra, killed their husbands on their wedding night.

Daphnis [Naiad]: Daphnis was a conventional name for a shepherd. Which Naiad, or wood-nymph, he loved is unknown.

Demeter: Ceres, the goddess of grain and crops.

Demophöon [Phyllis]: Deserted by this Greek hero, the Thracian princess Phyllis killed herself.

Dia: The island on which Ariadne was deserted (also called Naxos).

Diana: the virgin goddess of the hunt, famed for her beauty.

Dido: The queen of Carthage, she was in love with Aeneas, who deserted her to found Rome. She then committed suicide.

Dionê: Another name for Venus, though in some versions of the myth she is Venus's mother.

Dionysus: Another name for Bacchus.

Dirce [Amphion]: Amphion avenged his mother Antiope's death by tying her killer Dirce to a bull's horns.

Dodona: An area in Epirus, on the northwest coast of Greece.

Dolon: A Trojan spy killed by Odysseus and Diomedes.

Egeria: The wife of Numa Pompilius, second king of Rome.

Elysium: The Elysian Fields were the paradise of the underworld.

Enceladus: A giant with 1,000 arms (Ovid's invention?).

Endymion: The object of Luna's desires. He was granted perpetual youth—along with eternal sleep in a cave in Caria, in Asia Minor.

Ennius: A Latin author (239–169 B.C.E.), he wrote extensively in all genres.

Ephyre: The ancient name for Corinth.

Erato: The Muse of lyric and love poetry.

Eriphyle: The wife of Amphiaraus, bribed to send him against Thebes, where he died.

Eros: Cupid, or Love.

Eryx: A mountain on the western shore of Sicily, it was one of the many sites sacred to Venus.

Euphrates [Tigris]: Rivers in Mesopotamia (modern-day Iraq).

Europa: A young girl seduced by Jove in the form of a bull. He then swam far out to sea with her on his back.

Eurotas: A river in Sparta.

Eurytion: A drunken centaur who triggered the brawl at Pirithous's wedding feast.

Evadne: The wife of Capaneus, who died scaling the walls of Thebes.

Falisca [Camillus]: A Roman general, who in 360 B.C.E. subdued the town of Faleri (a Faliscan town) in Etruria (north of Rome).

Gaea: The goddess Earth, mother of the Titans.

Gaius: Gaius Caesar (20 B.C.E.–C.E. 4) was the emperor Augustus's grandson.

Galatea [Nereid; Nereus]:One of the 50 sea nymph daughters (Nereids) of Nereus, a kind of "old man of the sea."

Gallus: Gaius Cornelius Gallus (70–26 B.C.E.) was a highly connected political, military, and literary figure, influential in the development of love elegy. He apparently overstepped some bounds by boasting of his Egyptian campaign and was condemned by the Senate. He probably committed suicide.

Ganymede: The cup-bearer to Zeus. The name became synonymous with the generic office.

Gargara: A crest on Mt. Ida.

Gorgon: The mythical female monster at the sight of which one turned to stone.

Graecinus: A real (and highly placed) person, C. Pomponius Graecinus was suffect Consul in C.E. 16.

Gyas: A hundred-armed giant.

Harmonia: The daughter of Venus and Mars.

Hector: The prince and great defender of Troy, killed by Achilles.

Helen: The wife of Menelaus, abducted by Paris, prince of Troy and hence son of Priam. Her rape triggered the Trojan War.

Helicon: In Greece, the mountain home to the Muses.

Hercules (in the Greek, Herakles): A mythological hero who performed prodigious feats of strength and miraculous tasks.

Hermes: The Greek name for the Roman Mercury, the messenger god and conductor of souls to the afterlife.

Hermione: The daughter of Helen of Troy.

Heroides (the): Ovid's *Heroides* tells, in epistolary verse, the stories of numerous heroines spurned or abandoned by their lovers.

Hesiod: The author (fl. 700 B.C.E.) of the *Theogony* and *Works and Days*, poems on the birth of the gods and on the means to living an honest life, respectively. He came from Ascra in Greece.

Hippodamia [Pelops]: To win her hand, suitors had to best Hippodamia's father in a chariot race. To lose meant death. Pelops cheated and won.

Hippolytus: The son of Theseus, he was accused of adultery by his stepmother Phaedra, then killed by his horses when a bull from the sea panicked them.

Homer: A legendary eighth-century B.C.E. Greek epic poet, supposed author of the *Iliad* and the *Odyssey*.

Hylaeus: A centaur rival of Hippomenes.

Hylas: Hercules' boy-lover, abducted by water nymphs.

Hymen: The god of weddings and marriage.

Hymettus: A mountain southeast of Athens, it was famed for its honey.

Iasius [King Minos]: Ceres fell in love with the shepherd Iasius on the slopes of Mt. Ida. Minos was the king of Crete. When Ceres' daughter Proserpina was snatched away to the underworld by Hades (Pluto), Ceres refused to let the crops grow on earth. When her daughter was later allowed to visit her for some months out of the year, the crops returned and the cycle of the seasons began.

Ida: A mountain near Troy.

Ilia: Seduced by Mars, the Vestal Virgin Ilia was sentenced to death by drowning in the Anio. The river god pitied her and saved her.

Ilithyia: The Greek goddess of childbirth, sometimes considered as Diana.

Illyria: The northwest region of the Balkan peninsula, on the eastern Adriatic Sea.

Inachus [Melie; Bithynia]: A river god in Greece, Inachus was wed to Melie. Ovid's use of Bithynia, on the south coast of the Black Sea, is obscure.

Ino [Phrixus; Helle]: Their stepmother Ino tried to kill the twins Phrixus and Helle, but they were rescued by a flying golden ram. Helle fell off into the sea, bequeathing her name to the Hellespont.

Io: Juno turned this love object of Jove's into a cow.

Iole [Alcides]: An Oechalian princess of Thessaly, courted by Hercules ("Alcides").

Ionia: A region on the central west coast of modern-day Turkey.

Isis: The Egyptian goddess of the House of Life, she is sometimes depicted as a cow.

Janus: The two-headed Roman god of doors and gates (he faced both ways—like a door—on Roman coins).

Jove: The Roman father of the gods (the Greek Zeus).

Jupiter: Another name for Jove or Zeus.

Lais: Famous courtesan of Corinth.

Laodamia: The wife of Protesilaus, the first Greek to die at Troy (while stepping ashore), she committed suicide from grief.

Latium: Roughly, central Italy.

Leander [Hero]: A pair of legendary lovers. Leander swam the Hellespont to reach Hero, but drowned one night in the attempt. Hero then killed herself from grief.

Leda [Semele]: The sister of Helen, raped by Zeus in the form of a swan. Semele was visited by Zeus as a thunderbolt and was killed.

Lemnos: An Aegean island whose women, afflicted with the punishment of a sickening smell by Aphrodite because they would not honor her, killed their husbands, who had imported new wives from Thrace.

Lethe: The underworld river of forgetfulness and oblivion.

Liber: One of the many names for Bacchus.

Lightborn: In Latin, Lucifer means "light-bearer." The evening (and the morning) star, he is sometimes imagined as driving his chariot through the sky.

Linus: Apollo's infant son, torn to pieces by wild dogs.

Livia: Livia Drusilla (58 B.C.E.–C.E. 29) was the wife of the Emperor Augustus and mother of the Emperor Tiberius.

Lucifer: Literally, "lightborne," or "light-bearer"; the Morning Star, or Venus as the same.

Lucretius: A Roman poet (94–55 B.C.E.), author of the philosophic poem *On the Nature of Things*.

Luna: The moon.

Lycoris: Actually Cytheris, an actress and former mistress of Marc Antony's.

Lydia: An area in Asia Minor, directly opposite Greece across the Aegean Sea.

Macer: Pompeius Macer was a poet friend of Ovid's, and the Emperor Augustus's director of Rome's libraries.

Machaon: The physician to the Greek army at Troy.

Maenad(s): Frenzied female devotees of Dionysus (Bacchus).

Maenalus: A mountain in the heart of the Peloponnese.

Maeonia: Another name for Lydia. Homer's birthplace was thought to be Lydia.

Malea: A famously dangerous promontory on the southeastern coast of Greece.

Mantua: Birthplace of Virgil.

Mars: The Roman god of war (the Greek Ares).

Marsi (the): An Italian tribe noted for their spells and magic.

Medea: A Phrygian sorceress married to Jason, winner of the Golden Fleece. In revenge for his new marriage to Creusa, she murdered their two children.

Medusa: The snake-haired Gorgon killed by Perseus. Her look could literally petrify.

Megara: A Greek city south of Corinth.

Menander: A Greek comic playwright (fl. 315 B.C.E.).

Methymnia: A city on the northwest coast of the island Lesbos.

Midas: A king whose touch turned everything to gold.

Minerva: The goddess of wisdom, crafts, and arts.

Mt. Ismarus: In Thrace, it was the home of the great musician Orpheus, whose art could tame wild beasts and move stones.

Mulciber: Another name for the god Vulcan (also called Hephaestus), husband of Venus.

Muses: The nine deities devoted to the arts. They are often thought of as inspiring poet, historian, dancer, etc., respectively.

Myron: A famous Greek sculptor (fl. 450 B.C.E.).

Myrrha: She slept with her father, King Cinyras, and was turned into a myrrh tree. See Book X of the *Metamorphoses*.

Naso: Ovid's full name was Publius Ovidius Naso.

Nemesis [Cynthia; Lycoris]: These were the notional mistresses addressed in the love poetry of Tibullus, Propertius, and Gallus respectively.

Neptune: Ruling god of the sea and brother of Jove (Zeus).

Nestor: The venerable (and garrulous) Greek counselor at Troy whose name was a byword for old age.

Nike: The Greek goddess of victory.

Niobe: For bragging of her many children and insulting Latona for having only two (Apollo and Diana), she saw her own children slaughtered. She then turned to stone and wept eternal tears.

Nireus: A handsome Greek boy-soldier at Troy. In later tradition he was mentioned as Homer's Ganymede.

Nisus: A king whose daughter Scylla cut off a lock of his purple hair. He died, and she then betrayed his city of Megara to its besieger Minos, with whom she had grown infatuated.

Notus: The South Wind.

Numidia: Roughly, modern-day Algeria.

Nyctelian (the): Another name for Bacchus.

Orestes: The son of Agamemnon, he and Pylades were famous for their friendship. He avenged his father's death by killing his adulterous mother Clytemnestra. Aeschylus and Euripides both treat the subject in plays.

Orion [Side]: Orion the hunter lost his wife Side to Hades when Hera was insulted by Side's beauty.

Orithyia: The daughter of the legendary king of Athens, Erectheus.

Osiris: The Egyptian god associated with righteousness, the sun, and the Nile. Roughly equivalent to the Greek Apollo.

Palatine (the): One of the seven hills of Rome.

Pallas: Pallas Athena (Minerva), the goddess of wisdom. The olive was her sacred tree.

Paphos: A city in southwest Cyprus, it was the home to a temple sacred to Venus.

Paraetonium [Canopus; Memphis; Pharos]: These sites in Egypt were associated with the worship of Isis.

Paris: A prince of Troy whose abduction of Menelaus's wife Helen began the Trojan war.

Parthia: Roughly, northern Persia, along the eastern shore of the Caspian Sea.

Pasiphaë: The wife of Crete's King Minos, she had sexual relations with a bull and gave birth to the man-bull monster the Minotaur.

Patroclus: Beloved friend of Achilles.

Peleus: The husband of Thetis.

Pelion [Ossa; Olympus]: The generation of giants tried to overthrow Zeus by piling Mt. Ossa on Mt. Olympus, and Mt. Pelion on Mt. Ossa. A proverbial expression for over-reaching.

Pelops [Hippodamia]: Pelops, a skilled charioteer, courted Hippodamia by besting her father Oenomaus in a race. Suitors who lost, died.

Penelope: The wife of Odysseus. While he wandered far from his home in Ithaca, she stalled her "suitors" by testing them, demanding that they first string Odysseus's bow before they could marry her. All failed.

Peneus [Phthiotia; Creusa; Xuthus]: Peneus, river god and father of Daphne, is here connected with an obscure myth. Creusa was wed to Xuthus, and they raised Ion, a son of Apollo, in Phthiotia, a part of Thessaly.

Penthesilea: The queen of the Amazons, she was killed by Achilles.

Pergamum: Loosely, another name for Troy.

Phaeacia: A utopian island in the *Odyssey*.

Phaethon: Having been struck down by Zeus for driving Helios's chariot too near the earth, Phaethon was mourned by his weeping sisters, whose tears turned to amber.

Pharos: An Egyptian island at the mouth of the Nile, famous for its lighthouse.

Phasis [Jason]: Phasis was a town (and river) in the Colchis, the home of Medea. Jason was the Argonaut who won the Golden Fleece.

Phemius: The blind bard of the *Odyssey*.

Philitas: A poet of Cos (fl. 280 B.C.E.).

Philomel [Tereus; Itys]: The grisly story of Philomela, Procne, Tereus, and Itys was a favorite subject of antiquity. King Tereus raped his wife Procne's sister, Philomela, then cut out her tongue to hide the crime. Philomela, in captivity, wove her story into a tapestry and sent it secretly to her sister. Procne took revenge by killing her son Itys and feeding him to his unsuspecting father, Tereus. As the king pursued the two women, Procne turned into a swallow, Philomela a nightingale, and Tereus a hoopoe. Ovid tells the story in his *Metamorphoses*, Book VI.

Phineus: He blinded his two sons accused of adultery by their stepmother Idaea.

Phoebe: The daughter of Leucippus, Phoebe was carried off by Castor. Her sister Hilaira suffered the same fate at the hands of Pollux.

Phoebus: Apollo, the Greek god of healing, prophecy, poetry, and music.

Phrygia: A region of central (modern-day) Turkey.

Pieria: Region in Macedonia. Pieros was the father of the nine Muses.

Pleiads (Pleiades) [Kid]: The seven-starred constellation of November's rainy season. When the Kid set, stormy weather ensued.

Po: A river in northern Italy.

Podalirius: The physician brother of Machaon.

Pollux: A renowned pugilist whose Greek name was Polydeuces.

Pompey: Gnaeus Pompeius Magnus (106–48 B.C.E.), Julius Caesar's rival, had a colonnade built in 55 B.C.E. in the southern area of the Campus Martius.

Priam: The King of Troy. One of his sons was Hector, killed by Achilles.

Priapus: The Roman god of gardens and the phallus.

Prometheus: He stole fire from the gods to give to mankind and was punished by being chained to a rock and having his liver gnawed at each day by an eagle.

Protesilaus: The first soldier to die in the Trojan war, killed as he set foot on the beach.

Proteus: A deity of the sea who could shift his shape.

Pylades: A friend of Orestes.

Quirinus [Bacchus; Caesar]: Tall temples in Rome to Romulus (on the Quirinal hill), to Bacchus (on the Palatine), and to Julius Caesar (next to the Forum).

Remus: Romulus's twin brother. The two boys were reared by a she-wolf.

Rhesus: A Thracian king and Trojan ally. Odysseus and Diomedes killed him and stole his horses in a night raid.

Romulus: The eponymous ruler of Rome. His brother was Remus.

Sabinus: A poet and friend of Ovid's. He wrote replies to the *Heroi-*

des, including Ulysses's to Penelope, Hippolytus's to Phaedra, Aeneas's to Elissa (another name for Dido), Demophoon's to Phyllis, Jason's to Hypsipyle, and Phaon's to Sappho (who then dedicated her lyre to Apollo).

Samos [Delos; Naxos; Paros; Lebinthos; Calymne]: Aegean islands marking Daedalus's and Icarus's flight north and east of Crete.

Samothrace: An Aegean island associated with the rites of Ceres (the Eleusinian Mysteries).

Satyrs: Half-men, half-horses, like the centaurs, but less threatening. Much given to wine and sexual excess, they followed Bacchus.

Scipio [Ennius]: Publius Cornelius Scipio Africanus Major (236–183 B.C.E.), conqueror of Hannibal, had a statue of Quintus Ennius (239–169 B.C.E.), a Roman poet and playwright, placed on his tomb.

Scylla [Charybdis]: At the Straits of Messina, between Italy and Sicily, these two were proverbial dangers, a kind of "rock and a hard place." Scylla was a monster with sea snakes and vicious dogs for her lower parts, while Charybdis was a lethal whirlpool.

Scylla: The daughter of Nisus, king of Megara, she cut off the lock of her father's hair that the city's safety depended on and gave it to her love, the besieging general King Minos.

Scythia: A land that lay beyond the Black Sea.

Semiramis: Legendary queen of Babylon, famed for her beauty.

Seriphos: An island in the Aegean.

Silenus: The oldest Satyr.

Simois: A river near Troy.

Sirius: The "dog star" of deep summer.

Sithonia: Another name for Thrace.

Sophocles: A fifth-century B.C.E. tragedian of Athens (author of *Oedipus the King*, *Oedipus at Colonus*, and *Antigone*).

Styx: A river in Hades by which the gods swore their oaths.

Sygambri: A Germanic tribe, they were defeated by Rome in 11 b.c.e. Their shorn hair was made into wigs.

Syrtes: Sandbars off North Africa, famous for their danger.

Tagus: A Spanish river famous for its gold.

Tantalus: He was condemned in the afterlife to perpetual hunger and thirst. Standing in a pool, he would bend to drink, only to have the water recede. If he reached for fruit on a branch above his head, it would draw back. Hence, "tantalizing" for "tempting" or "teasing."

Tarpeia: The legendary Tarpeia threw open the gates of Rome to the Sabine army, demanding as her price "what they wore on their arms"—gold cuffs. They killed her with the weight of the shields they bore. The Tarpeian rock was the execution site for Roman traitors.

Tatius: The Sabine king who attacked Rome after the rape of the Sabine women, then ruled the city jointly with Romulus.

Tecmessa: A Mysian princess taken captive by Ajax at Troy.

Tenedos: An island off the coast of Asia Minor, it figures prominently in the *Aeneid*.

Thais: A courtesan and Alexander the Great's mistress.

Thamyras: A bard blinded for having challenged the Muses to a singing match.

Thersites: A scurrilous, whining figure in the Greek camp at Troy.

Theseus [Ariadne]: A king of Athens who abandoned the Cretan princess Ariadne, who was enamored of him. She had helped him kill the Minotaur.

Thessaly: Northeast of Greece, its coastline borders the Aegean Sea.

Thetis: A sea nymph or Nereid, she hid her infant son Achilles to save him.

Thrace: Northeast of Greece, it borders Greece's northern neighbor, Macedonia.

Thrasius [Busiris]: A Cypriot seer to King Busiris of Egypt, he advocated sacrificing a human being to end a drought, and Busiris obliged by making him the first victim.

Tibullus: Roman elegiac love poet (55–19 B.C.E.)

Tiryns: Argolid city, the birthplace of Hercules.

Tityos: A Titan (of the generation of gods before the Olympians), he was condemned to have his liver eaten by vultures in the underworld. He had tried to rape Leto.

Triton: The son of Neptune, he could control the waves by blowing on the sea shell that was his trumpet.

Tyre: City on the Phoenician coast noted for its purple dyes.

Tyro: Daughter of Salmoneus; she fell in love with Enipeus, a river god in Thessaly.

Ulysses: The wily hero of the Greeks at Troy, he wandered for ten years before returning to his home in Ithaca. The *Odyssey* is his story (where he is "Odysseus").

Umbria: Roughly, central Italy.

Varro: A great Roman poet and scholar (116–27 B.C.E.), author of hundreds of works on history, farming, and the Latin language.

Varro: Publius Terentius Varro Atacinas (82–35 B.C.E.), a Roman poet, translated the Greek poet Apollonius Rhodius's *Argonautica* into Latin.

Venus: The goddess of love and mother of Cupid.

Verona: Birthplace of Catullus.

Vesta: Goddess of the hearth. The flame in her temple had to be kept going because it symbolized the life of Rome.

Via Sacra: Literally, "holy street/road/way." It was a thoroughfare noted for its shops of luxury goods.

Virgil: Publius Virgilius Maro (70–19 B.C.E.), author of the *Aeneid*, Rome's foundational epic. He wrote pastoral (the *Eclogues*) and agricultural (the *Georgics*) verse as well.

Vulcan: God of the forge. A blacksmith, he is Venus's husband, crippled by a limp.

Xanthus [Neaera]: In a somewhat obscure myth, the river Xanthus (Scamander) loved the nymph Neaera.

Zephyr: The West Wind.

Zeus: Greek father of the gods.

ACKNOWLEDGMENTS

No translation stands sui generis. In the course of these versions of Ovid, I have had the benefit of much help, both from other translations, and from suggestions by poet-friends; all infelicities are of course my final responsibility. I wish to thank Rhina Espaillat, Bill Coyle, Mike Juster, Deborah Warren, and all the members of the Powow River Poets. Special thanks as well to Jody Bottum, who first published II.14 of the *Amores* in *First Things*, and James R. Burns, who published I.1, I.4, I.5, and II.1 of the *Amores* in *Other Poetry*. And extraordinary thanks to Michael Schmidt of *PN Review* and Carcanet Press, which boldly saw the entire *Ars Amatoria* into print at *PN Review* over the course of three separate issues.

But beyond all these, I am grateful for the diligent and perspicuous attention to these lines by Betty Rose Nagle, whose scholarship and good sense saved me from many a flaw. I owe her an enormous debt.